Dear Jorge,

With deep appreciation for your
support, with best wishes,

[signature]
Jany 28/2010

The Fragile Forest

inside Brazilian Amazonia

The Fragile Forest
inside Brazilian Amazonia

Front Cover:
Main photo: The Amazon Rainforest & the River
Inserts (L-R): A Riberinho Girl, A Jaguar;
Victoria Amazonica Leaf; Dolphins in the Amazon;

Back Cover:
Acái Palm trees in the background

Text & Photos © 2010:
D.K. Bhaskar

Edited by:
Sumana Mukherjee

Design & Printing:
www.parishree.com

Published by:
International Fine Art Gallery
406, 8th Street, Augusta, GA 30901, USA
Tel: +1 706 826 1897
Fax: +1 706 826 4827
Email: valledolmo@att.net

First Print: 2010

Printed in India

Dedicated to
My Parents
&
Yadvinder Malhi

Foreword

Mr. Jose Vicente Pimentel
Former Ambassador for Brazil in India
New Delhi

As John Ruskin observed, poetry is the suggestion by the imagination of noble grounds for the noble emotions. By that standard, D.K. Bhaskar's *"The Fragile Forest: Inside Brazilian Amazonia"* is no doubt a poetic book. His photographs unveil the beauty of the forest, a feast to the eyes, as well as its mysteries that stirs strange apprehensions. They provide emotional clues that bring us closer to the majesty of the Amazon.

The Amazon is indeed beautiful, mysterious and majestic. Its dimensions are spellbinding. The region as a whole measures almost 5 million square kilometers. In Brazil alone, it covers about 3.5 million square kilometer- all of India would fit in this area.

And of course there is the river, which contains one-fifth of all the fresh water in the world, all of it in its massive dimensions measuring 7200 KM in length, with an average width ranging from 2 to 30 kilometers. Literature already features descriptions of 1,550 species of fish living in its stream. Thousands more have not been documented.

In the Amazon, there is a close relation between plant and animal kingdoms. Unlike, Asian forests, where the main pollinating and seed dispersion agent is the wind, over there pollen is carried by insects, and seeds area mainly dispersed by birds, small rodents, monkeys, other animals. During an experiment carried out in the 70's with a view to making an inventory of Amazonian insects, the total number of insect species on earth was upgraded from 10 to 30 million.

People commonly think of the Amazon region as one vast plain, wholly covered by an exuberant mantle of forest. It is not so. In fact, the Amazon region shelters savannas, plains, mountains, dunes, and many other variations, classified in 112 ecosystems. But the dominant figure is the forest itself.

The Amazon is closely linked to the chemistry of the atmosphere. The jungle gives off as much oxygen as it consumes. So it is far from being "the lungs of the world". What is more, this giant is weak. What is amazing is the fragility of the tropical jungle, where every form of life walks on a tight rope. It is somewhat difficult to believe at first sight; the vegetation is home to so many animal species, and it adapts so well to

the climate, that the jungle seems to be infinite and indestructible. It is not. All of this lushness teeters between a poor and acid soil, a scorching sun and an implacable rain of ultraviolet rays, never obtaining the respite known as winter.

For millions of years, Amazon wildlife learnt to master the art of self-preservation and recycling. This, while creating unlikely partnerships as a means of surviving in a hostile environment. In order to compensate for the poor soil, plants seem to have made a deal with an army of microorganisms capable of rapidly decomposing dead branches and freeing nutrients for their roots, which are also good at searching for food.

A number of associations among "specialists" of an animal or vegetable type turn the forest yet more fragile. If one species disappears, all the others related to it are also affected, and may vanish. A good example is the Brazilian nut. When it was planted commercially outside the jungle for the first time, the trees flourished, but produced no nuts. Eventually it was discovered that pollination of the blossoms depended on a tiny wasp that lived among the leaves of an orchid, which grew on other forest trees, though not on the Brazil nut tree. In other words, to cut down the forest surrounding a Brazil nut tree will prevent it from producing its fruit.

Much of the Amazon is still unexplored, and the lack of knowledge gives rise to misunderstandings. The weak of heart will tend to think of the worst. That is why movies and television disseminate the Amazon's reputation as a green hell, populated with horrendous monsters, piranhas, anacondas, and terrifying spiders. The sensationalist press and mass media make huge profits by airing news featuring accidents and catastrophes, burning, deforestation, massacres of Indians, pollution of rivers and so many other fantasies about the destruction of the "lungs of the world". Predictably, these alarming statements infiltrate once in a while the agenda of round table discussions that, even when well intended, do nothing to preserve the Amazon, because they are off the mark to begin with. It would certainly be wiser to see it, and try to understand it, before one makes an opinion about it.

Bhaskar renders great service in this regard. His passion for the Amazon wildlife comes through very clearly, and very beautifully. His work, which I hope the readers will enjoy as much as I do, does not solve the mystery of the Amazon, it rather suggests new mysteries for our imagination to dive into. These pictures can be likened to poetry. As I still say, Bhaskar's camera speaks from the heart, and conveys a powerful message.

However, if a picture is worth a thousand words, Bhaskar's book can also be favorably compared to many voluminous, but arid works on the Amazon. It suggests, by the imagination, the noblest grounds for our noblest emotions.

Embassy of Brazil
New Delhi   JOSE VICENTE PIMENTEL

The Negro-Branco area hosts diverse plant communities, including seasonally flooded and non-flooded tall, evergreen lowland forests reaching up to 40m in height, as well as low, evergreen flooded palm forests, which reach only 20m in height.

Trees in the Rio Negro basin typically grow to more than 40m in height.

Contents

A Caboclo family

Prologue

"The unsolved mysteries of the rainforest are formless and seductive. They draw us forward and stir strange apprehensions. In our hearts we hope we will never discover everything. We pray there will always be a world like this one. The rainforest in its richness is one of the last repositories of that timeless dream."

- E. O. Wilson, The Diversity of Life, 1992

Massive silting at the mouth of the Amazon has created Marajó Island, the largest river island in the world.
Much of the island is watered by rain, leading to radical modifications through agricultural development.

The Amazon rainforest harbours our planet's most diverse ecosystem. The expanse of the river and the adjoining rainforests continue to throw up many unanswered questions because there is much about the Amazon that we still haven't discovered. After four visits spread over 150 days and years of researching the region, I firmly believe it would take several lifetimes to uncover the truths of this magnificent rainforest.

A barely explored paradise of natural history, these forests pose numerous challenges for modern science. From being a sink for environmental pollutants produced by developed countries, to being the target of massive destruction of trees for timber, the Amazonian land faces many complicated threats today.

Equally intriguing are the people of Amazonia. Their lives, cultures, diversities and co-existence with the wilderness make them a remarkable people to study. As a result, this geographical region not only interests ecologists and environmentalists, but also anthropologists, historians, geographers, geologists, economists, tourists and photographers.

This book is a celebration of the spirit of the Amazonian rainforests. It aims to introduce the reader to the mystery and romance of the Amazonia, supported by photographs shot over multiple visits. While every attempt has been made to bring alive the Amazonian landscape, this book is not intended to be a detailed historic, economic, scientific or geographic reference.

The Fragile Forest: Inside Brazilian Amazonia is a humble attempt to bring out some fascinating facts about the life and soul of Brazilian Amazonia as I have experienced it. The visual exuberance of the land and the warmth of the people of Brazil won my heart – and I hope my photographs will bring home some of that warmth and colour to you.

Colourful ornamental fish species are aplenty in the Amazon. Yet there is little regulation or monitoring of their survival or trade, valued at $100 million annually.

On a morning walk along the mouth of the Amazon river, I saw this beautiful Caboclo girl.

BRAZIL

Capital   :   Brasília

Area   :   8,511,965 sq km

Coastline   :   7491 Km

Population :   As per 2000 census: 186,112,794

Religions   :   Roman Catholic (nominal) 80%, other 20%

Languages :   Portuguese

GDP   :   5.1% (2004 est.)

Currency   :   Reals

São Paulo and Rio de Janeiro are among the largest cities in the world.

Flag of the Republic of Brazil

A tram in Rio's old town

A colonial Portuguese church
in Pelourinho, Salvador

The Iguazu falls

Brazil

The Country
and its People

"We shepherded the night as though she were a bevy of girl
and we guided her to the ports of dawn with our staffs o
rum, our unhewn rods of laughter."

- Jorge Amado (1912-2001

Brazilian novelis

A street carnival in Rio de Janeiro.

*M*odern-day Brazil is an intriguing amalgamation of the numerous peoples it has absorbed over the centuries. It has emerged as a country of innocence, beauty, charm, warmth and humour, buoyed by its high-spirited population.

Covering more than 8,00,000 sq km, Brazil is the largest country in South America – encompassing about half the continent – and the fifth largest country in the world. A predominantly Christian society with 184 million people, Brazil is a vibrant mosaic of colours, flavours, sounds and diverse communities.

The 27 states of Brazil are conventionally divided into five regions. The North, the largest of the five zones, is entirely covered by the Amazon rainforest. In the North-East lies the coastal belt, while the world's largest wetland, the Pantanal, accounts for most of the West-Central region. In the South-East lie the major cities of São Paulo, Rio de Janeiro and Belo Horizonte, while the South is home to most of Brazil's immigrant communities. The country has 44 national parks to safeguard and showcase its mountains, beaches, flood plains and mangroves.

Pantanal, the largest wetland region in Brazil, has a diverse collection of aquatic plants.

Brazil shares its borders with 10 countries – all the South American countries, in fact, except Chile and Ecuador – while its Atlantic coastline extends to more than 7,300 km. The Equator crosses the northern region of the country through Macapá, well-known to football fans as home to the Zerão, the only ground in the world with two halves in two hemispheres. The Tropic of Capricorn runs through southern Brazil, close to São Paulo. Ensconced between these two important lines of latitude, Brazil enjoys an enviable average temperature of 20ºC throughout the year.

The Portuguese brought with them their African slaves and capitalized fully on the gold rush of the 18th century. As word spread of their wealth centres around the country, Brazil saw the arrival of the Japanese, Chinese, Africans, Germans, Koreans, Italians, British, all travelling thousands of miles in search of power, opportunities and riches. Each people brought with them their individual cultures, traditions and customs. The successive waves of migrants, however, augured ill for the land's indigenous tribes: From well over 1,000 at one time, they were reduced to about 200 tribes at the beginning of the 21st century.

A country of settlers, Brazil was colonized by the Portuguese in the 16th century. Legend has it that a Portuguese explorer by the name of Pedro Alvares Cabral set sail for India via the Cape of Good Hope. Hopelessly lost, he landed on what he thought was an island, which he christened Ilha de Vera Cruz (Island of Vera Cruz). Once it became clear that this was no island, the name was changed to Terra de Santa Cruz. Several changes of name later, the country finally came to be known as Brazil, after the native brasil wood tree, which yielded a red dye popular in Europe.

Beachside high-rises, backgrounded by a favela (shanty town) to the right.

The Corcovado mountain, shot from atop the Sugarloaf mountain.

A peek into the modern history of Brazil reveals that its economy depended first on timber, then on sugar, followed by gold, rubber and coffee in that order. During World War II, when the import of manufactured goods was hit badly, Brazil turned towards modernization to sustain itself and its economy. This was followed by three decades of industrialization, from the 1940s to the 1960s. With this came urban development, railways, industries, telecommunication, networks and, unfortunately, national debt. Changing leadership and wise economic strategies have made the 21st century Brazil an industrially competent country. Yet there is a great deal of disparity between the rich and the poor, a social reality that will perhaps take generations to sort out. Besides, the education system in the country faces a serious crisis, with many young wealthy citizens turning to more prosperous nations for quality education and the poor unable to afford any at all.

Despite its colonial past, turbulent modern history and current social disparities, Brazil has evolved into a strong, adaptable nation. The people make all the difference to the spirit of the nation. Their liveliness and energy, their optimistic nature and instinct to live and enjoy themselves despite adversity make for an incredible experience for a visitor. Their dance, music, carnivals, cuisines and beverages reflect an irrepressible culture and an incredibly resilient society.

No account of Brazil is complete without touching upon football, a national passion. The beautiful game is played and followed even in the remotest parts of this huge country. It is common to find little children dribbling and maneuvering the ball along beaches and on the streets. The land football legends like Pelé and Ronaldo call home, Brazil is a sight to behold on the evening of a national team victory. No wonder then that the world is already looking forward to Rio hosting the 2016 Olympics !

In a country where football makes the world go round, Pelé is still king.

If football is Brazil's perennial passion, its annual passion is Carnaval. Held every year ahead of Lent, the Christian period of mourning – *carne vale* literally means farewell to flesh/meat – the parades in Rio are street operas in every sense of the term. Over two nights, 12 samba schools compete with each other to present the most captivating float, usually built around an aspect of life in Brazil that could include Michael Jackson or climate change as well! The schools pull out the stops in presenting their creative vision through their choice of themes, costumes and dancers in a tradition that dates back to 1723.

Over the years, the number of spectators has grown to mammoth proportions: An estimated 500,000 people converge on Rio from across the world to cheer the tableaux and party with the millions of Cariocas – as anyone born in Rio is known – in arguably the sexiest celebration on earth.

Among the most important roles of the carnivals is that of the *porta-bandeira*, the woman in charge of the samba school flag. The percussion-based samba music gives participants the rhythmic liberty to sing, dance and work the parade simultaneously in a style known as *batucada*.

Alongside the main parade in the Sambadrome, in the heart of Rio de Janeiro, and various balls around the city, the beach and various neighborhoods host their own miniature versions of the street festival.

Costumes are elaborately hand stitched for the carnival.

Grand celebrations during the annual Rio de Janeiro Carnaval at Sambádrome.

Sliver Beaked Tanager.

The Green Iguana.

Blue-and-Yellow Macaw.

Sobralia pulcherrima

White necked Jacobin

Golden headed Tamarin

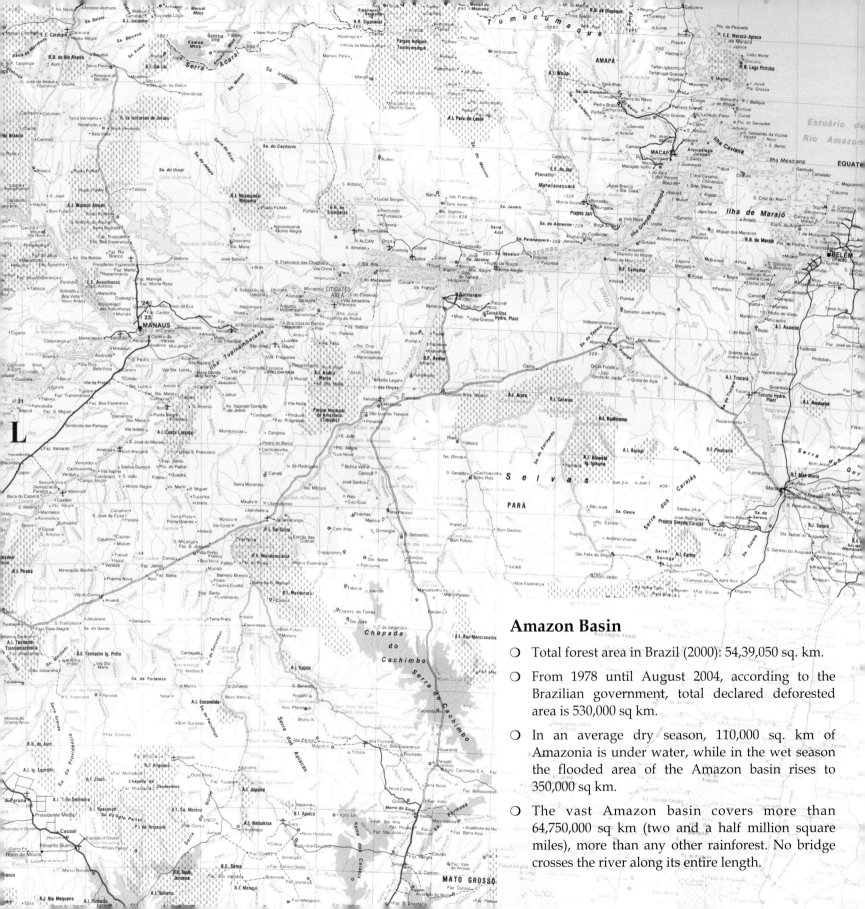

Amazon Basin

❍ Total forest area in Brazil (2000): 54,39,050 sq. km.

❍ From 1978 until August 2004, according to the Brazilian government, total declared deforested area is 530,000 sq km.

❍ In an average dry season, 110,000 sq. km of Amazonia is under water, while in the wet season the flooded area of the Amazon basin rises to 350,000 sq km.

❍ The vast Amazon basin covers more than 64,750,000 sq km (two and a half million square miles), more than any other rainforest. No bridge crosses the river along its entire length.

Jaguar

Paradise Jacamar

"It should not be believed that all beings exist for the sake of the existence of man. On the contrary, all the other beings too have been intended for their own sakes and not for the sake of something else."

- Maimonides

The Guide for the Perplexed 1:72, c. 1190

The Marvels of the
Amazon Basin

In the Amazon, palms are the cornerstones of many environments, and intricately woven into the cultural fabric of both rural and urban peoples.

MYSTICAL and alluring are two of the many adjectives associated with the Amazon basin. The mighty Amazon river – also known as the Marañion (in Cordillera, Peru: the name comes from the Spanish explorers' question Mar o No, sea or not), the Solimões (from the Peru-Brazil border to Manaus, where it merges with the Rio Negro) and the Amazonas (from the confluence to the Atlantic) – flows through thousands of miles of dense forests, sheltering innumerable species of plants and wild animals. The Amazonian rainforests comprise about one-third of the South American continent. The drainage basin of the Amazon accounts for much of this area, but it also includes parts of the Orinoco river basin in the north and of the Tocantins river basin in the east.

Though the Amazon is usually associated with Brazil, the Amazonia also covers parts of Ecuador, Bolivia, Peru, Venezuela, Colombia, Guyana, French Guiana and Suriname. Thirty-three percent (3.6 million sq km, an area larger than the entire continent of Europe

Moss grown on an abandoned leather shoe, indicating the region's high humidity.

excluding Russia) of these forest lands lie in northern Brazil.

A flight over Brazil invariably makes for magnificent views of the rainforest: One can see miles and miles of uninterrupted greenery crisscrossed by the sinuous Amazon and its tributaries. The Amazon basin has 1,100 tributaries, 18 of which are more than 1,600 km long. The river network, more than 80,000 km long in all, accounts for 17 per cent of the world's fresh water.

Meandering through the rainforests, the Amazon periodically floods much of the land along its banks. Consequently, the shoreline vegetation is completely submerged in water for seven to 10 months a year. The average depth of the Amazon during floods is 30-50 meters; at other times, it is about 15-40 meters. Only in two places – the Lower Rio Negro and the Middle Rio Amazonas – does the river touch a depth of 100 meters. Scattered all along the banks of the river are boathouses, small huts and settlements of indigenous Indians or mixed races, indicative of the extent to which the original inhabitants became one with the rainforests.

A Caboclo girl.

*A Caboclo dwelling along the river. Their
lifestyles are adapted to the rainforest.*

Am·a·zon (ăm'ə-zŏn', -zən): In Greek mythology, the Amazons were a tribe of warlike women who lived in Asia Minor. Their name is supposedly derived from the Greek a-mazos, meaning 'without a breast' because, according to the legend, they cut off their right breast so as to be better able to shoot with a bow and arrow. The Amazons lived in a matriarchal society, in which women fought and ruled while men performed the household tasks. Over time, an Amazon came to describe a strong, aggressive woman. So, when the early Spanish explorers on the river encountered a fierce, defensive people – including some female warriors – they named it after the Greek tribe of yore.

Multiple layers of vegetation in the rainforest prevent rain from

The Amazon near Santarém, some 3000km from the Andes, carries most of the sediment load that is eventually delivered to the Atlantic, a further 800km away. Muddy water is often called 'white water' in the Amazon basin, though in other parts of the world the term refers to rapids.

The geological events leading to the formation of the Amazon basin began around 80-90 million years ago, when dinosaurs still roamed the earth. First of all, flowering plants appeared in the supercontinent we call Gondwanaland. The plants created favorable conditions for the evolution of tiny insects and other diverse life forms. Second, the splitting of Gondwanaland caused South America and the African continent to drift apart from each other and from South Asia, Australia and Antarctica.

The splitting of the continents led to a third important event about 15 million years ago: The rise of the range of mountains we now call the Andes. Prior to the formation of the Andes, the proto-Amazon river – as geologists refer to the original river that existed before these seismic events – initially flowed from east to west. The Andes effectively stymied the river's course to the Pacific Ocean, thereby creating the largest lake and swamp ecosystem on earth. During the Ice Age 2.4million years ago, when sea levels dropped, the lake drained out rapidly, creating the world's largest river system with the principal river – the Amazon – flowing west to east.

The Amazon is known for its many different hues and characteristics. Soon after being born in the Apacheta cliff in the Nevado Mismi (5,597 m) in Arequipa in the Peruvian Andes, 700 km from Lima, the young river carries Andean sediments and suspended solids, which gives it a *café au lait* color. Further into the Brazilian and Guiana highlands, the muddy Amazon is joined by the clear waters of tributaries such as Xingu and Tapajo. Many tributaries are born not in the mountains but in the forest, giving rise to waters that are clean yet dark, because of the presence of huge amounts of incompletely decomposed organic matter. The most famous of these 'dark tributaries' is the mighty Rio Negro.

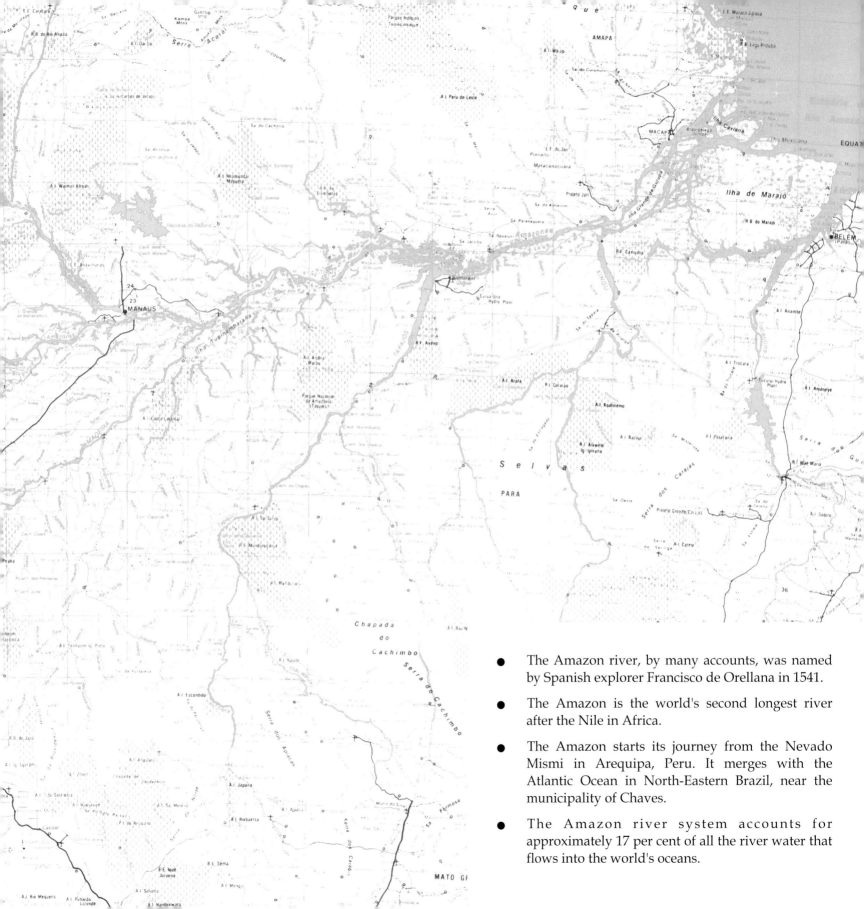

- The Amazon river, by many accounts, was named by Spanish explorer Francisco de Orellana in 1541.

- The Amazon is the world's second longest river after the Nile in Africa.

- The Amazon starts its journey from the Nevado Mismi in Arequipa, Peru. It merges with the Atlantic Ocean in North-Eastern Brazil, near the municipality of Chaves.

- The Amazon river system accounts for approximately 17 per cent of all the river water that flows into the world's oceans.

The moisture-saturated environment of the rainforest can almost classify it as a wetland.

The blending of white waters, clear waters and dark waters makes for the planet's largest river by volume. The Amazon accounts for one-fifth of the fresh water annually discharged into the oceans by all the world's rivers – that is, five times that of the Congo, 10 times that of the Mississippi and 3,500 times that of the Thames. More than 100 billion litres of water flow into the Atlantic every minute, diluting the salinity of the ocean for more than 100 miles offshore. During floods, the Amazon adds nearly 150 thousand billion litres of water to the Atlantic per second.

Belém stands on swampy ground, on the banks of the Amazon estuary, watered by the Tocántins, Guamá, and the Amazon.

Life beneath the water is as abundant and diverse as in the surrounding rainforest. The floodplains can be under water up to 40ft deep for as long as 10 months. But many species manage to maintain their metabolism and retain their foliage over this time, having adapted to low oxygen availability.

Biodiversity: Extensive yet elusive

It is impossible to put an exact figure to the number of plants and animals that the Amazonian rainforests nurture. New species of life continue to be identified in these forests even as the world voices its concern at the alarming rate of deforestation and habitat-loss. By some estimates, the Amazon basin accounts for 20 per cent of the world's plant species – there are more than 30,000 flowering plant varieties here making it the world's richest eco-region.

However, because there are several layers of vegetation beneath the tree canopy – besides a dense carpet of foliage at the ground level and a deep leaf-litter layer – any sighting of wildlife is rare and fortuitous. This element of uncertainty only heightens the rainforest's mystery and awe-inspiring appeal.

A large variety of fungi are found in the Amazonian rainforests. Although fungi are not plants, they play as important a role in the local environment, breaking down dead plant matter and releasing nutrients for use by live plants.

The terra firme forest in the Caxiuanã region of Eastern Brazilian Amazonia, along the Xingu river, is an upland forest area with closed vegetation, an average 35m-high canopy, some emergent trees 50m high and a 450-550 plant species density per hectare.

There are two types of rainforests: temperate and tropical. Temperate rainforests are found along the coasts in the temperate zone (parts of the world that receive between 60 and 200 mm of rainfall annually, where temperatures reach a summer high of 32°C and fall below freezing in winter). Tropical rainforests are dense, humid and wet areas clustered around the Equator between the Tropic of Cancer (23.5° North) and the Tropic of Capricorn (23.5° South). Tropical rainforests comprise only 20 per cent of the world's total forests, covering 6.7 per cent of the earth's land surface. Yet half the world's plant and animal species live in these rainforests.

Most of the Amazon's biodiversity is found in or depends on the rainforest canopy. The canopy is the dense ceiling created by closely spaced trees, while the understory beneath the canopy is formed by more widely spaced, smaller tree species and juvenile individuals.

The Amazon rainforest consists of four layers of vegetation or communities: the emergent layer, the canopy, the understory and the forest floor. The emergent layer comprises trees – some of them more than 60 meters tall – that tower above the canopy. The leaves in this layer are small and have a thick waxy surface ideal for trapping water. Wind pollination of the winged seeds propagates these trees. The majority of fauna that inhabits this layer – eagles, macaws, harpy eagles, marmosets, woolly monkeys – finds everything they need to survive here and so almost never leave their habitat.

The canopy is the most important layer of the rainforest. Most canopy trees have smooth oval leaves with pointed tips that allow water to drain off quickly. The canopy filters out about 80 per cent of the sunlight. Millions of epiphytes (parasitic plants that draw their nutrients from already established plants) thrive here.

The understory, which is about three-and-a-half meters high, receives only two to five per cent of the available sunlight. This shadowy layer supports many unique plants, which have remarkably dark green leaves adapted to harvest maximum sunlight. Most plants in this layer are insect- or animal-pollinated. The largest concentrations of insects inhabit this layer.

The forest floor is the lowest layer of the rainforest, receiving only about two per cent sunlight. This layer is almost devoid of any plants but it is a rich source of organic, decomposing matter. Most nutrients for the trees are made available by this layer.

A flooded forest and water lilies illustrate the complex beauty of aquatic habitats in the world's greatest river ecosystem.

The floating meadows shrink during the low water season. When the river floods, they form very productive habitats and provide cover and food for many animal and plant species.

Named after Queen Victoria, the Victoria Amazonica is the most famous and the largest of all water lilies, with leaves sometimes over two-and-a-half meter in diameter on stalks six to seven meters in length.

South American wildlife includes 45 species of turtles: Four are land turtles (tortoises), six are marine turtles, while the rest are freshwater turtles. The yellow-spotted river turtle is one of the largest of its kinds.

In terms of diversity and number, insects are the most successful inhabitants of the rainforests. The Amazonian landscape is home to nearly 3,000 species of fish, 125 species of snakes and around 350 species of mammals, including the world's biggest otter. *(For an exhaustive list of species, see attached booklet.)*

More than 90% of the animal species found in the rainforest are insects whose life histories are intimately linked to trees, ferns, orchids, bromeliads and other epiphytes. A single square mile of rainforest often houses more than 50,000 insect species.

In the neotropics, bats provide critical ecosystem services, including pollination and seed dispersal. Seen here is a sharp nosed bat.

The Scarlet Ibis, endemic to the Amazon,
lives on fish, frogs, reptiles and crustaceans.

The Amazon provides the perfect environment for amphibians. Abundant insect life – read food – and water for reproduction make for ideal living conditions for a large number of different species. The humid climate suits their permeable skins and the warm temperatures allow activity day or night. Frogs and toads are more frequently heard than seen in the Amazon, but their chorus adds a uniquely tropical ambience to the Amazon night.

The Amazonian rainforests harbour more species of reptiles than anywhere else on earth. It includes, but is not limited to, tortoises, caimans and turtles. The anaconda, the world's most feared snake, is synonymous with the Amazon. It is rarely seen, as it is secretive and spends most of the time underwater. It feeds on fish, small turtles, caimans, capybaras, tapirs and wading birds.

With more than 1,800 kinds of birds – or one-third of the world's total known bird species – it is no exaggeration to describe South America as a bird continent. The bird diversity is an amazing 125 species per hectare, including seven kinds of colorful macaws and five of kingfishers. The rainforest also houses hundreds of dainty and delicate hummingbirds; their population is considered a valuable testament to the variety of flora, since they thrive on the nectar of a large number of flowers. The most exotic bird is undoubtedly the toucan. This handsome bird, with its colourful bill, tops my list of the marvels of Amazonian bird life.

The Anaconda, a member of the boa family, prefers to live in swamps and sluggish streams. With an average length of 20ft, an average diameter of 12inches and an average weight of more than 150kg, it uses the water to escape predators and to conceal itself while searching for food.

Silky anteaters are yet another species unique to Amazonia. Feeding only on ants and termites,
they can adapt themselves to live in many different kinds of habitats, including grasslands and dense forests.

Monkeys make up one of the important groups of arboreal mammals in the rainforest: 30-odd species are found here. In early 2009, a new species, Mura's tamarin, was found in a remote part of Brazil, and was immediately put on the imperiled species, because of habitat loss. Pictured here: A squirrel monkey.

Sloths are the slowest
creatures of these rainforests.
To compensate for their lack of
speed, they grow a layer of
blue-green algae on their fur
that camouflages them in the
greenery. They have highly
developed adaptations for
feeding on leaves.

The jaguar best describes the spirit of the Amazonian rainforests. The largest cat and the top territorial predator in the western hemisphere, they are most closely related to the Asian tiger, but are only found in the New World. They have a powerful and compact body, and a robust head. For millennia, jaguars have served as potent cultural icons for many indigenous American people, from the Mayans and Incas to the Guarani Indians of the Gran Chaco.

Brazil's Flooded Forests Earn World Natural Heritage Site Status

A core area of the Amazon rainforests was awarded World Natural Heritage site status by UNESCO in 2000; the area was expanded to include the Jau National Park in 2003. Vast sections of the sprawling forests have been earmarked as sites of utmost ecological value. A few of these include the Amanã Sustainable Development Reserve, part of the Mamirauá Sustainable Development Reserve, Anavilhanas, Amanã, Jaú and Mamirauá Conservation Units. A World Heritage Site designation means that the site is considered important for humanity and, for that reason, will have access to special sources of funding for its preservation.

The capybara is the world's largest rodent, which feeds on a large number of aquatic grasses and floating plants. It is highly prized for its meat in the Amazonian flood plains. The manatee is the Amazon's largest aquatic mammal, capable of staying under water for an hour before surfacing to breathe. Like capybaras, manatees, too, are targeted by Amazonian fishermen and hunters because of the reported aphrodisiacal qualities of its meat.

Every true traveller dreams of sailing down the Amazon. It requires patience
and perseverance, but the wealth of Amazonia more than makes up for it.

The sun sets over the Pará river as a boat leaves
Belém for the Caxiuána National Forest.

An Indian in the
Amazonia

"Is it lack of imagination that makes us come to imagined places, not just stay at home? Or could Pascal have been not entirely right about just sitting quietly in one's room? Continent, city, country, society: the choice is never wide and never free. And here, or there . . . No. Should we have stayed at home, wherever that may be?"

-- Questions of Travel by **Elizabeth Bishop** (1911-1979)
American poet

The Amazon rainforest has a huge live collection of flora species. Botanical experts say 2.5 acres of the forest can yield 700 different species of trees and twice that number of plants.

On one of my return flights from Brazil, looking down on the ever-intriguing landscape from my airplane window, I experienced that rare feeling of coming full circle. Growing up on tales of the Amazon as a child in India, I had nurtured dreams of exploring the rainforests. Later, even as my acquaintance grew with the Indian jungles, I carried with me a niggling dissatisfaction about the paucity of accessible, verifiable knowledge about the Amazonian forests.

And now, as I gazed at the boundless greenery before my eyes, I silently said thanks that my prayer had been answered – and experienced a new humility that however much we could aspire to learn about the Amazon, there would always be something new for the forests to teach us.

Say Brazil and the commonest association is with Péle, the legendary football player hailing from this nation, and the Samba, the country's iconic dance form. But Brazil is much bigger than football, dance or even coffee. As home to the world's largest rainforests fed by the Amazon river, it's anyone's guess which one is mightier, the river or the forest.

The Amazon rainforest is a reality check that assures us that nature still has depths that man's greed cannot overcome. Given the extent to which it is unexplored even today, it both invites and warns the adventurer who sets out to 'conquer' it. As for the river, it overwhelms one and all with its silent power. Not only is it the widest and most voluminous river on the planet, it is one of the top two longest rivers – the other one being the Nile.

The sense of wonder that will accompany me throughout Brazil sets in early. It is 7am when I clear the customs formalities at the São Paulo international airport but, without any Portuguese, it is tough to locate my connecting flight to Belém, where my Amazonian adventure was supposed to begin: All the signboards are in Portuguese! After hours of encountering courteous "English, sorry, no", I finally run into a charming young girl, an Argentinian also travelling to Belém. She speaks fluent English and I stick with her till Belém, the gateway to the Amazonia.

At Belém, Luiz, my only contact in Brazil, is waiting for me, much to my relief. Post-breakfast – a feast of Amazonian fruits like pupunha, acerola, cocona, aquaje for this vegetarian – we go on a short tour of the city, whose roads, people, architecture, vendors remind me of Chennai and Mumbai. Sipping a tender coconut, I get my first glimpse into the attitudinal habits of Brazilians: From crossing roads without waiting for the lights to change, to extended luncheon hours and from rolling down car windows to say hello to a familiar passer-by to slipping out of their shirts when the weather gets too warm, everything speaks of a people at ease with themselves and the world.

For all the apparent laidback spirit, however, Belém has an industrious trading history. Located to the north of Brazil in the state of Para, its wealth comes from rubber, nuts, cocoa, jute and timber. No surprises there: The city of 2,000,000 is surrounded by the rich rainforests and its lifeline is the Amazon itself.

Tropical fruits from the Amazon basin. Rainforest locals apparently eat more than 2000 of the 3000-plus varieties of fruits found here.

The refurbished warehouse by the riverside, `Estacao das Docas'.

The Ver O Péso Market on the riverfront in Belém.

Hammocks are the best mattresses for an adventure into the Amazon rainforest.

The river is the road of the Amazonia, conveying everything from cows to coconuts and people to pins in the long, narrow indigenous boats.

Residents of Belém, like all Brazilians, love to sing, dance and drink at all hours. So I do not wonder that at 6pm, when our cruise boat is all set to leave for the Caxiuãna national forest, music has been playing at full blast for an hour on board. I am excited and enthusiastic about the adventure ahead, but feel a bit isolated because of my inability to converse in Portuguese. Before long, however, a co-passenger enquires if I want to join in the dance. Soon, my inhibitions disappear. A few of members of our team – I am travelling with a group of researchers and scientists from Brazil, Suriname, Venezuela, Peru, USA and the UK – sip Brazilian beer while others look for a place on board to string up their hammocks. Yes, much to my amazement, everybody sleeps on hammocks – or, rather, lives in them. I am advised to pick up a hammock for myself at a roadside stall, while the boat is still docked.

A free-spirited, uninhibited people, Brazilians also love their dance, music and coffee.

By the time the sun is setting, we are well into our 643 km journey to the Caxiuana national forest, located between the cities of Belém and Santarém. As the boat glides forward at 25 nautical miles per hour, the dance on the top deck picks up. Everyone pitches in, playing their own tunes and songs. I opt to sit next to the captain to soak in my first views of the river and the forests. As we move deeper into the Amazon and lose sight of one bank, I think we could well be on an ocean. The might of the river simply overwhelms me.

Soon the moon throws its milky white shroud over us, but the music doesn't show any sign of easing up. I wonder if the decibel levels do not disturb the wildlife around. But then again, even they are Brazilian! The dancing resumes after a sumptuous dinner of rice, beans and meat and it is well past 4 am when we sleep. The hammocks are tied next to each other, sometimes above another. The throbbing of the diesel engine becomes part of the background noise, but before long the insects take over.

In the morning, I am awake by 5.40 am, waiting for the sun to come up, much to the captain's amusement. Exotic parrots, macaws, swallows and tits are busy with their morning chores. A wagtail catches my attention in the front of the boat, whirring its tail with its customary energy. As interesting are the Riberinhos, the river people who live right on the edge of the Amazon in brightly coloured huts. Women and children look on as we cruise past, the kids waving vigorously at us from their little row-boats.

The scarlet macaw is a large parrot that thrives in the emergent and canopy layers of the Amazon rainforest. Like other parrots, it is a seed predator.

Kids elsewhere may learn to ride a bicycle or rollerskate, but in the Amazon,
Caboclo children learn to maneuver a canoe to go to school or visit a neighbour.

The Amazon is a busy waterway. Huge boats use the Amazon to ferry cars, industrial accessories and move commodities from place to place. Though the river is largely calm, in some places the going can be rough. More than 50 boats go up and down all the way to the cities of Santarem and Manaus every night. As we sail, I notice the river changing colour from brown to green to black. I learn later that the colour is determined by the composition of sediments and organic matter in that particular spot.

The Amazon is not just about the vast jungles, but also the teeming human life on either side of the river.

Mention of the Amazon may conjure up images of a wild land and an untamed river, but almost the entire river system witnesses a continuous stream of boats and human activities.

As the sun sets, four pink dolphins pop up and display their gymnastic skills, each time somehow eluding my camera. Different species of birds wings their way back home as we, too, near our destination. A journey of almost 27 hours on this mighty river, along some of the most pristine rainforests of the world, comes to an end with frogs orchestrating a welcome recital on the boat jetty. This is the most memorable boat journey I have ever undertaken, but much more adventure lies in store for me in the jungles of Caxiuanã.

Just for an idea of the vastness of the Amazon rainforest: It is four times larger than the next two tropical forest regions: Congo Basin and Indonesia.

The national forest is a 33,000 sq hectare section of the Amazonian forest, located on the west bank of the Caxiuanã Bay, which was created by rising sea waters at the end of the last Ice Age. These forests have some of the tallest trees in the region, with canopy heights exceeding 50 metres. The density of the tree species here is approximately 200 per hectare. I feel dwarfed by their imposing presence. The air is still and humid, whatever be the time of the year, but the whole ambience is fresh and invigorating.

While the relatively dry July-August is the preferred season for visiting Caxiuanã, the noise one makes navigating the dry leaf-strewn forest floor is enough to scare away any wildlife. Moreover, little light penetrates through the dense canopy, making it difficult to sight – let alone photograph – any wildlife.

The greater yellow-headed vulture is a large bird that prefers undisturbed tropical forests to open habitat.

At one point, we spot vultures hovering over the canopy and I decide we have to go to the spot. Taking precautions not to step on any snakes, we make our way through the vegetation, ignoring the occasional sudden movement on the edges of our vision, and are rewarded by the sight of a huge vulture landing on a tree-top.

I must admit that I feel extremely fortunate to have witnessed scores of action-packed moments in this unexplored wilderness. Among one of my strongest memories are the pair of yellow eyes of a fierce harpy eagle staring at us, its claws and beaks still bearing evidence of the brown-bearded saki monkey it had just killed. We stand mesmerized at a distance as it consumes its prey before taking off.

Trees have to compete with their neighbours constantly. With more than 80 per cent of the forest's food being produced in the canopy, trees tend to shoot up quickly, developing very straight narrow trunks and few low branches.

There are around 20 species of piranha in the Amazon, with only four or five posing any danger to humans. In fact, it makes for one of the favourite meals for those sailing on the river.

The Amazon abounds in fish, which is also a staple for the locals. The piranha, a famous culinary delicacy, is also a dangerous fish to tackle. Although many exaggerated stories exist about their man-eating instincts, the reality is that these events are extremely rare. At the most, they only manage to nip the fingers of unsuspecting fishermen. Along the river, it is commonplace to see canoes with a big catch of this predator, which is eaten along with tucanars (another popular edible fish) by fish-loving Amazonians.

Cavianhā is a forestland adjoining the Caxiuanā forests. This pristine wilderness reverberates with curious echoes as we land. I am told this is the first time in recent history that any human being was setting foot in these forests. Excitement, apprehension and curiosity crowd my mind as I follow my researcher-friends onto this sacred ground. This, I think, is perhaps how heaven was meant to be !

At scores of points along the river, banks open out to form natural beaches, perfect settings to catch a fish, set up a barbeque and party with friends.

Most boatmen are adept at using arrow heads for fishing.

Interestingly, no predator has evolved to exploit all three of the Amazon river system's aquatic habitats: river channels, flood plains and streams. Yet, each one of the habitats has a characteristic top predator.

Cavianhã is rich hunting ground for piranhas. While here, I witness the traditional way of fishing piranhas with a spearhead. Every day around sunset, our boatman – born and bred in the Amazonian jungles – anchors his boat near the shore and flashes his indigenously designed torch on the waters. The moment he glimpses a shoal of fish underwater, he aims his spearhead, and gets his fish, never missing once. Early man must have fished in much the same way, I think.

After a couple of nights of time standing still in Cavianha, a speedboat carries us to a small town called Breves, six hours away. We cross muddy waters and narrow streams to reach this town, which is also a major army base. With a population of not more than 15,000, Breves can be said to be the essence of the Amazonia, nurturing much of the original local lifestyle. Boats, ranging in size from huge freighters to modest dugouts, leave for different destinations from Breves, carrying everything from foodgrain to footwear. Ports such as these serve as docks for much of the trade and commerce of the Amazonia.

A part of Marajó Island is dominated by floodplain forest subject to inundation by tidal changes.

Gliding below the rich green of the Amazonian canopy, keeping one's eyes peeled for the occasional pink dolphin or a scarlet ibis, or releasing a sigh at the quick succession of floodplains and the savannah is one thing, but an aerial view of the flooded forest is a different experience altogether. On an enchanting canopy tour over the Amazon in a four-seater aircraft, I see magnificent vistas of the flooded forests and a part of the world's biggest river island, the Ilha de Marajó. I spot flocks of green, yellow, pink and even violet birds, and water buffalocs grazing and wallowing in the vast flood plains. At the end of the tour, I look over a beautiful, undisturbed bank, with the river lapping furiously at the shore. The trees sway to the tune of the wind as my pilot maneuvers a large turn and begins our return journey. This is surely an adventure I did not want to end soon.

Marajo island is famous for its elaborate vases, colourfully decorated ceramic artifacts used for domestic, funerary and ceremonial purposes.

Caboclos of all ages paddle primitive dugout cascos (canoes)

My last tour in the Amazonia takes me to Chaves. The landing strip at Chaves is nothing but an uneven grassy patch and the aircraft wobbles so much I am not sure if we will be able to really get off the plane. I am struck by the simplicity of the so-called airport, where a platform and a wooden welcome arch constitute all the infrastructure. It's impossible not to fall in love with this cute landing strip and airport!

Chaves' claim to fame, obviously, lies elsewhere: This is where the Amazon merges with the Atlantic Ocean. People of this little village are a mixture of different races. I am told that deep inside the adjoining forests a clan of Amerindians still resides. How exciting, I think, my mind recollecting stories of the heroic native Indians that I had heard in my childhood.

Needless to say, I have only scratched the surface of the Amazon basin. It will take many more dedicated explorers to uncover the secrets of this mysterious land. It remains my life's ambition to return to the Amazonia and experience some more of its evergreen splendour.

On my way back from Brazil, looking down on the stupendous landscape from my plane window, I am exhilarated to have undertaken this journey. It had taught me many valuable lessons about nature's grandeur, its plentiful ways, about the joys of simple living, and about man's unthinking selfish ways.

However, the Amazon being Amazon will ultimately win. Or so I hope.

River levels fluctuate periodically between 17ft and 33ft all along the Amazon basin. Raised houses in the lowest reaches of the forest offer some respite.

Roman Catholicism, brought to Brazil by Jesuit missionaries and observed by the first Portuguese settlers, is the primary religion of the country.

Science
& Research

By Yadvinder Malhi

The best friend of earth and of man is the tree. When we use the tree respectfully and economically, we have one of the greatest resources on the earth.

- Frank Lloyd Wright (1867-1959),
American architect and educator

Dr Yadvinder Malhi reads the sunshine sensor fitted on top of the Caxiuaná tower to measure incoming radiation.

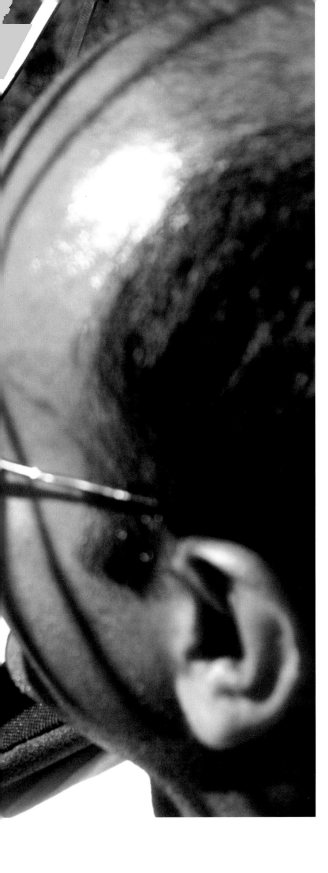

𝒯he Amazonia first seduced me in 1995. I had come to the city of Manaus, in the heart of the Brazilian Amazon, for a short term project to measure the exchange of carbon dioxide between the rainforest and the atmosphere. However, it took a month for my equipment to go through the importation procedures and, in the meantime, I had plenty of time to browse through the library and archives of the National Amazon Research Institute (INPA) in Manaus. I remember that my eye was continually drawn to a map of the Amazonia on the library wall. On that map, Manaus was just a small label in a vast sea of green, larger than India, larger than the European Union. And in that vast green sea, there were none of the usual signs of dense human civilization and almost no roads - just two large cities, a few medium-sized towns, and scatterings of small settlements. Instead of roads there was a fine network of rivers, whose names resonated with the rhythms of exotic languages - Tupi-Guarani, Gê, Ticuna and many others. I was used to the dense settlement maps of places like Europe and India, where nature reserves are jealously guarded as islands lapped by expanding human activity. Yet, here was something different: An ocean of green that reminded humankind of its smallness in the big picture of things, a vast blank map that reminded me of how much there was still to be learnt and discovered. I could not have felt more excited and awed if I had landed on another planet. In fact, I had landed on another planet, vast, green and wild. In those early months in the Amazonia, the course of my life changed, and I knew that I would spend my life attempting to unravel just a few of the secrets of the tropical forest and its relevance to the Earth. I knew that in my life I would only at best unravel a few secrets while the great forest of mysteries sat before me, but the process of discovery would be an act of devotion itself to this great green goddess.

Researchers measure tree growth in the plotted area of the forest. When the girth of the tree expands, researchers can collect invaluable data on the soil, tree competition and rainfall patterns in Amazonia.

In the years since that moment, I have been lucky to see the Amazonia from many viewpoints; from its birth point in the high Andes of Peru, amidst the steaming volcanoes of Ecuador, in the company of the jaguar in Bolivia, in lovely riverside towns in Peru and Colombia, in the bustling cities of Brazil, in the ravaged forest and settlements of the frontier, amongst the meandering snake-like rivers of the west and the vast, lake-like rivers of the east, and at the Amazon's muddy exit into the Atlantic Ocean, where the river first announced its huge presence to early European explorers by the presence of muddy but fresh river water far out in the ocean. These journeys have been conducted with the aim of understanding what determines the presence and structure of this forest, the role this forest plays in the global atmosphere, and how both climate change and deforestation will affect the forest and the planet.

The vast biodiversity of the Amazonia has fascinated researchers and continues to be explored and described, but only in recent decades have scientists begun to venture beyond the description of diversity to an understanding of the influence Amazonian

ecosystems have on the regional and global environment. Scientific understanding of the global influence of the Amazonia has advanced hugely in the last decade, thanks largely to a Brazilian-led project, the LBA (Large-Scale Biosphere-Atmosphere Experiment in Amazonia). In this project, Brazilian scientists have demonstrated how newly industrializing countries can lead the way in understanding and protecting their natural heritage, in partnership with industrialized countries but very much in control of their own destiny. And in doing so, they can be more effective than an army of outsiders. The threats to the Amazonia are many, but the Brazilian government, civil society and science are fully engaged in debating these issues and debating the future of this vast region. The future of this magic land is still far from clear and there is much to fight for, but Brazil is to be applauded for engaging seriously with this issue.

We have gained many new insights into the role that the Amazonia plays in global climate. For example, we now understand that the deep roots of the trees here ensure that the forest releases water to the atmosphere throughout the dry season, ensuring that the region stays humid and wet. Without these deep roots, the region would suffer much more severe seasonal droughts. When forest areas are converted to (shallow-rooted) grassland or agriculture, the vegetation no longer has access to deep roots, and seasonal droughts can increase in intensity. This affects not just regional but global climate. Being at the Equator, the Amazonia is one of the great engines of the global circulation of the atmosphere, which is driven by warm, moist air rising over the Equator and sinking at higher latitudes. Hence changes in the water supply of the Amazonia can change climate patterns in distant lands. Computer simulations and weather analyses suggest that rainfall patterns in lands as distant as North America, Europe and Central Asia are affected by the Amazonia.

Another surprising discovery is how dust-free the atmosphere over Amazonia is. Most tropical land regions are now dusty, hazy places, as the skies over India before the monsoon can attest. Oceans tend to be much cleaner, except when they are immediately downwind of land areas. Yet recently, scientists have discovered that the tree cover over the Amazonia keeps the air as clean as it is over the ocean, so much so that the region has been nicknamed "the green ocean". This feature affects not only air quality but also the nature of rainfall. Clean air tends to produce warm, gentle rain, dusty air

Large scale deforestation and illegal mining are a constant threat to the survival of this ancient forest.

produces more extreme rainfall with violent thunderstorms (this is why the first rains of the Indian monsoon can often be the most dramatic).

We have also learned much about the ecology of tropical rainforests. The immense productivity of the Amazonia is a result of its perpetually warm and wet climate, not of its soils. The soils of most tropical forests are poor, being washed of their nutrients by millions of years of heavy rain and high temperatures. Hence we face a paradox: how does such productivity and green biomass thrive on such poor soil? The answer is that the forest ecosystem has slowly accumulated nutrients from the soil and atmosphere over the millennia, but holds them not in the soil, but in the living and dead biomass of the forest itself. When a leaf falls to the forest floor it is entangled in roots and fungi within a few days, thus ensuring that the nutrients released from the decaying leaf are rapidly recycled, rather than being lost to the soil and washed out into the rivers. The tragic consequence of this is that once the forest is removed, there may be enough nutrients in the soil to allow agriculture for a decade, but soon the land becomes impoverished and often abandoned. Even if the land is abandoned, it can take decades or centuries for the forest to recover. Hence the great forests of the Amazonia sit on a fragile base; the great size of the trees often does not indicate the fertility of the forest but the longevity of the trees. For example, some large trees in the Amazonia have recently been dated to be more than 1,000 years old.

My own work, both in Brazil and in other places, has concentrated on understanding how these forests will respond to global climate change. The Amazon forest is a great store of carbon in biomass and soils, and the release of this carbon could potentially accelerate the rate of global warming. Alternatively, an increase in this carbon store could slow down the rate of global warming. Working together with collaborators in the UK and in South America, we have discovered that the dynamics of the carbon store have changed in recent decades. Trees in the forest appear to be both growing faster and dying faster. This may also be causing changes in the composition of the forest, with vines and other fast- growing plants increasing at the expense of slow-growing plants. We are still trying to puzzle out exactly why this happening, but the fact that is occurring across the Amazonia and in other regions, suggests that the cause is global and not local. One possible suspect is that the rising amount of carbon dioxide in the atmosphere caused by fossil fuel burning is causing a change in the biology and dynamics of forest trees. The long-term consequences of these changes are far from clear, but we have learned that the forest is a dynamic and ever-changing place. The Amazonia, home to a quarter of our planet's biodiversity, is a major actor in the drama of planet Earth, and yet its role is still mysterious, and we still have much to learn.

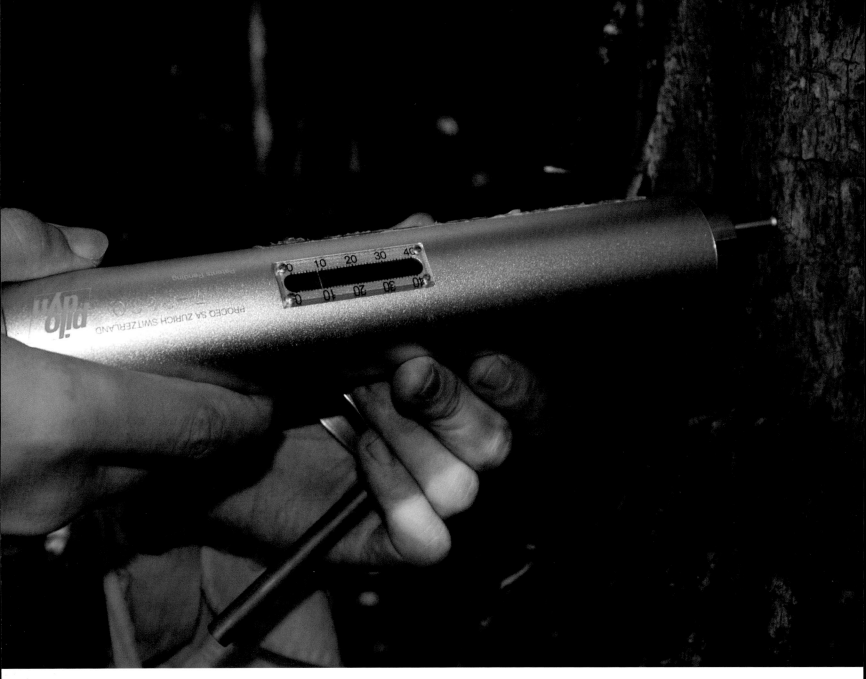

Jerome Chave, researcher from French Guyana, testing wood density with a Pilodyn instrument.

Climate Change and the Amazonia

by Oliver Phillips

All across the world, in every kind of environment and region known to man, increasingly dangerous weather patterns and devastating storms are abruptly putting an end to the long-running debate over whether or not climate change is real. Not only is it real, it's here, and its effects are giving rise to a frighteningly new global phenomenon: the man-made natural disaster.

- Barack Obama, *US President*

The quantum of sediment released by the Andean tributaries muddies the Amazon river from the foothills to the Atlantic, thereby blocking sunlight and inhibiting the production of phytoplankton and other algae.

*T*he Amazon forest is vast and magnificent. So huge in fact that you can fly over it for hours on end, with nothing below you but a seemingly endless carpet of green, interrupted here and there by winding, giant rivers and small ox-bow lakes. Sometimes the rivers are coloured milk chocolate by the mud that washes off the towering Andes to the west. Sometimes they are crystal-clear. And sometimes they are like black tea, stained by the tannins washed out from a billion leaves.

The sun glints back at you from these watery surfaces, and it is easy to imagine that it was like this, and always will be.

Yet the forest is changing, and often in ways not immediately obvious to the human eye. One-fifth of the Amazon rainforest has been destroyed. While there are some signs that deforestation can be controlled, the destruction is undeniable, and more subtle changes are occurring too. Where the big mammals and birds are hunted out for food, the trees that need these animals to disperse their seeds will continue to fruit year after year but their seedlings have little chance of surviving under their parent's shade: Hunting, eventually, can kill tree species as effectively as animals. A changing climate can also silently kill too, as we will discover below.

But there are reasons for hope too. One of these is that people are realizing the valuable role that forests play in our climate – not only do they recycle huge amounts of water and bring rains that feed crops even beyond their borders, but they also store huge amounts of carbon (100 billion tons of it, to be precise, in the Amazon, to the nearest 10 billion tons or so), so keeping it out of the atmosphere. This benefits us all. It also appears that for decades now trees in the forests that remain have actually been growing bigger, taking up an extra half-billion tons of carbon each year. In fact, over recent decades, tropical forests worldwide have absorbed one-fifth of global fossil fuel emissions. In several ways then, nature is doing us all a big favour in helping to slow climate change.

The question is – for how long? Climate change means that it is likely that the Amazon (like most of the world) will become hotter this century. It may also become drier. While plants may well be able to deal with extra heat, if the great Amazon water-cycle becomes disrupted and droughts intensify, they may well find it harder to cope. Our research team of more than 60 scientists has worked throughout the Amazon for years, and now we have the first solid evidence that drought can cause big massive carbon losses in tropical forests, mainly through killing trees.

We based our study on the unusual 2005 drought in the Amazon. This gave a glimpse into the region's potential future climate, in which a warming tropical North Atlantic may cause hotter and more intense dry seasons. By measuring thousands of trees for years before the drought and then through the event itself, we were able to discover how they responded to the unusual conditions.

The 2005 drought reversed decades of carbon absorption in which the Amazonia has helped to slow climate change, because it killed lots of trees. Yet, in fact, to the eye most of the forest appeared as before – tree death did accelerate but not enough to affect the complex structure of the forest. Only by examining the records from dozens of plots did we discover an increase in the death rate of trees. So, at the small scale of each plot the effects were modest, but because the region is so vast, these small ecological effects can scale up to have a large impact on the planet's carbon cycle.

The 2005 drought helped as a natural experiment in the present situation. That was a short, sharp drought, and also showed significant increase in mortality with drying, and was evidence that the stronger the drying, the greater the increase in mortality. In normal years, the forest absorbs nearly 2 billion tons of carbon dioxide. The drought caused a committed loss of more than 3 billion tons of CO2, principally by killing trees. The total impact of the drought was therefore approximately 5 billion extra tons of carbon dioxide in the atmosphere.

A few species were especially vulnerable, including some important palm trees which couldn't get enough water to feed their huge leaves. This means that as well as releasing carbon, we can expect drought to have some subtle but important effects on the forest's plant and animal species too. No other ecosystem on Earth is home to so many species. If we fail to stop climate change, much of the forest itself may remain, but the complicated fabric of life which underpins it will certainly change. Some species will gain. Others will lose, and many adapted to the wettest areas may find themselves with nowhere to go.

Yet the biggest danger to the Amazon is probably not climate change. It is not even hunting, or logging and agriculture and the deforestation which accompanies it. Rather it is the combination of climate change plus development: A drier forest is a vulnerable forest but it will still be a forest unless it burns. And fires, set to clear land for farming, can escape out of control in a drought. Amazon trees evolved without fire and so they have none of the protective features – like thick bark or heat-resistant seeds – which their relatives in areas which burn naturally have evolved. Once burned, the canopy thins, dead wood accumulates on the ground, the hot tropical sunlight pours in, and the whole system is primed to burn again.

To keep the Amazonia standing in a changing climate will require better ways of living in the region, without the use of fire

Blackwater rivers are not confined to the Amazon basin. Blackwater is essentially tea brewed in areas where plant compounds are not completely decomposed. The Rio Negro (Spanish and Portuguese for black) is the second largest tributary and sixth largest river in the world.

especially. Other models exist already. Using mixtures of compost and charcoal, indigenous peoples have managed to turn patches of nutrient-starved tropical soils into artificial, rich 'black earths' that can yield bountiful crops in small farms. The push of industrial farming into forests is driven by some unlikely forces – including the meat that we eat (many cows eat soya grown in the Amazon), and the cars that we drive (... palm soil... sugar cane....); with knowledge and action these forces can be reversed. And, last but not least, if we can find ways to reward those countries that help us all by keeping their climate-protecting forests intact and standing, the Amazon and its millions of species may still have a bright future. It is in all our interests to do so.

How the Amazon responds this century is still very unclear; as well as the uncertainty in the climate models themselves, their future depends in part on how trees respond to the increased temperatures (e.g. drought experiments only alter the moisture supply), and how well the Amazon nations are able to control the ignition of droughted, and therefore fire-vulnerable, forests.

The soil quality in some parts of Amazonia is very poor as heavy rain washes away nutrients continually. Yet vegetation thrives and continues to evolve. Scientists are still working to understand soil dynamics here.

As the Sun sets, the nocturnal Amazonia comes to life.

Ribeirinhos have been living on the banks of the Amazon since the time of the rubber boom, eking out a living through subsistence fishing and small garden plots that grow bananas, beans, corn, manioc and watermelons.

The Caboclos are descendents of European rubber harvesters who were brought in by merchants to collect natural rubber from the forest. They eventually married into the local populace. Their children, commonly known as Ribeirinhos or river-dwellers, mostly live in the river-front dwellings along the Amazon and its tributaries and run the small commerce on the river.

Sustaining
the Amazonia

The future of mankind can be assured only if we rediscover
ways in which to live as a part of nature, not apart from her.

- Prince Charles of England
at Copenhagen Climate Summit, 2009

Boats ply like taxis between small towns and large ports.

ne of the biggest advances in conservation is the idea that the natural world (ecosystems such as forests, grasslands, and wetlands) provides all sorts of 'hidden' benefits to the communities that live close by. This concept is called 'ecosystem services' to reflect the idea that the natural world provides goods and services – much like the post office or an energy company – to humans. These services include things such as pollinating crops, providing water for crops and livestock, and preventing erosion. It also includes some less obvious things such as medicines derived from plants and the provision of a resource that people from all parts of society can enjoy.

Scientists have split up the goods and services provided by ecosystems into different categories. The Millennium Ecosystem Assessment (2003) suggests four main divisions: provisioning services, regulating services, cultural services and supporting services. These services are really important for understanding why the forest ecosystem (and other ecosystems) is so valuable, and why we need to conserve it.

Provision Services

These are the products obtained from nature that include food (food products derived by plants, animals, and microbes) and fibre (material such as wood, jute, hemp, silk, etc.). These products are not just for eating. This category also contains biological material that serves as sources of energy (e.g. firewood); or that is important because of the genetic information it contains. It also includes plants and animal products used in natural medicines and pharmaceuticals, and even ornamental 'resources' such as a beautiful orchid or a colourful tropical fish. Another very important provision service is the fresh water that is essential to all forms of life – including humans.

Regulating Services

These represent all the benefits that the ecosystem provides in terms of the regulation of ecological processes – for example, the maintenance of air quality through

The acái palm is one of the Caboclos' primary sources of livelihood. They work quickly to gather the palm berries because the quality of the fruit deteriorates within 24 hours of plucking. The berries are loaded into traditional baskets called lata and transported to Belem to be sold.

photosynthesis and respiration. Natural ecosystems contribute chemicals to the atmosphere influencing all aspects of the air. Even local changes in the type of land use (e.g. chopping down forest to grow crops) can have a long-term impact on rainfall patterns and the temperatures of the region. Other types of regulating services include: water regulation (that helps avoid

Black corn

flooding); erosion control (vegetation can prevent landslides by holding the earth together); water purification and waste treatment (many ecosystems can help to filter and decompose organic wastes); regulation of human diseases (changing an ecosystem can alter the abundance of disease carrying animals such as mosquitoes or rats); and pollination.

Cultural Services

These very interesting services can be defined as the non-material benefits that people obtain from the natural world. Examples include the spiritual enrichment that you get from communing with nature, the enjoyment of sports such as fishing, hiking and birdwatching, or the simple and relaxing pleasure of visiting a natural place and seeing all the wonderful plants and animals that live there. Nature has also provided inspiration for great art and architecture, and provides beautiful landscapes that everyone can enjoy. This service is also the basis of ecotourism, a very important business in some of the poorest parts of the world.

Supporting Services

Our final category refers to the services that are necessary for the production of all other ecosystem goods and services. These services are different from the others because they are indirect services or occur over very long time periods. Examples would include the formation of soils, water cycling, nutrient cycling, and the production of oxygen, among others.

Thus, all natural ecosystems, such as forests and rivers, are really important for humans.

The Amazon rainforest, the biggest in the world, provides many ecosystem goods and services that benefit everybody, from the communities of Indians who live deep inside the forest to people all over the world. The easiest services to be recognized are the production of wood, cattle, soya, Brazil nuts, etc. However, there are also other services that we normally forget to take into account, such as the pollination of crops or the control of flooding of one of the biggest rivers in the world, the Amazon.

Other very important services also include the maintenance of the amazing diversity of species that draws people from around the world to visit or study the forest. A service of global significance is the role of the forest in taking up carbon dioxide from the atmosphere – this gas is one of the main causes of global warming and, if the Amazon forest is cut down, the global climate would change dramatically. Similarly, the regulation of the water cycle helps control the weather for the whole of South America. Even though the forests of Amazonia provide all of these vitally important benefits and services, it is still at risk due to human action. The region suffers from widespread deforestation for timber or to create new farms, urbanization, large scale extraction of mineral products, etc. and all these cause changes in the ecosystem. If this widespread disruption of the ecology of the forest continues, we may lose some of the services that we depend upon so much. Therefore, everybody needs to do their best to help to conserve the forest!

Top: A boy with a catch of fish at the mouth of the Amazon
Below: Buriti, one of the edible fruits of the region.

Tall Tree Stories:
The Canopy

By Meg Lowman

I think that I shall never see a poem as lovely as a tree.

- Alfred Joyce Kilmer (1886-1918),

American poet

Wide canopies keep the wind from penetrating to the forest floor, which are almost preternaturally still. Forest floor visibility extends to just 25- 30 feet.

*D*uring the 1970s, tropical rainforests were scientifically considered a "black box" (translation: a big, dark region full of the unknown). How many species exist on our planet? What lives in the tops of tall forests? Why don't those millions of beetles eat up all the foliage? How do tropical forests control the climate and lifestyle we enjoy in the temperate zones? As a young graduate student, armed with a tolerance for leeches, mud, and smelly socks, I wanted to solve the mysteries of tropical jungles. In order to study tropical trees, I needed to climb to reach their foliage. So I packed some ropes, a harness, climbing hardware, camera and notebooks into a rucksack, and headed for the jungles of Australia.

My career has been unconventional: I climb trees for a living. I feel fortunate that I was never knocked unconscious by a falling cannonball tree fruit, nor bitten by an Australian brown snake, and never fell from a tall tree (just small ones!). I first voyaged to Australia some 30 years ago to study the tropical forests of this "lucky country", in part because no one had ever studied rain forests Down Under. Only an estimated five percent of the original Australian rain forest had escaped the chain saws by 1978. I had to hurry.

In trying to find something important to study, I realized that almost ninety five percent of every tropical tree was both out of sight and reach. In essence, these jungle canopies were never seen, much less studied. I sewed my first harness and carved my first slingshot to rig my ropes, and set my sights on exploring at the top. I have never looked back (or down, in this case). From Australia, I took my harnesses and ropes to Peru and Brazil, falling in love with some of the world's most mysterious yet important rain forest canopies.

E.O. Wilson of Harvard University characterized forest canopies as the last biotic frontier on Earth. Tree crowns escaped scientific exploration in the past for the simple reason that the logistics of overcoming gravity were never solved. Charles Darwin was allegedly hoisted in a chair by South American natives to view the canopy, just as a novelty. Some 150 years later, I was fortunate to become one of the first explorers into this uncharted frontier, and remain awestruck by each and every return voyage out on a limb. The canopy is home to the greatest number of species on Earth, now considered a hotspot for biodiversity. Current scientific literature estimates that our planet houses up to 100 million species, of which almost half live in the treetops (and many, not surprisingly, are insects!). Forest canopies are centres for photosynthesis, for foods and medicines, for flowering and fruiting, and for growth, so it is logical that animals will tend to live up there amongst the sunlight and foliage.

Initially, my biggest challenge was to design safe methods to reach the treetops. I spent long hours becoming adept with a slingshot and propelling my fish-line through a safe passage up and over a strong branch. More recently, I designed treetop walkways for public visitation (including wheelchairs in some cases) in Florida and also in the Amazon. Once these field access methods were designed and tested, the stage was set to solve the biological mysteries of these aerial ecosystems hidden just above Earth: the treetop inhabitants and their interactions; and the dynamics of growth, death, productivity and diversity. In essence, what makes these complex systems function, and how can we insure their stability for future generations?

The jungles of Peru, representing the upper regions of the mighty Amazon river and its tributaries, are my

Scientists and their assistants frequently need to climb tall trees for data and sample-collection. A tropical rainforest canopy contains a range of dangers – from venomous reptiles, stinging insects and thorny plants to lightning, sudden winds, cold rain and unbearably hot conditions.

favorite rainforests on Earth. The amazing emergent trees such as the great kapok tree (*Ceiba pentandra*) and the cedralinga (part of the legume family, but certainly much larger than a green bean plant!) are not only challenging to climb but they also house enormous numbers of species undescribed and poorly understood. It is, in some ways, a race against the chain saws, to discover and document the biodiversity of the Amazon, before it disappears – and, even more important, it is critical to seek solutions for conservation as well as for the livelihoods of people who live there. One site downriver from Iquitos, Peru, named ACTS (Amazon Centre for Tropical Studies) is operated by the Explorama tourist lodge, and has a canopy walkway almost half a km long. This is a great place for students to learn about Amazon rain forest canopies.

My own research in the Amazon deals with herbivory (definition: consumption of foliage by animals). I spend hours and months and years as a leaf detective, measuring how much foliage is eaten by consumers and trying to figure out who is doing all the munching! This interaction of plants and (mostly) insects relates directly to ethnobotany, which is the science of how plants are used for medicines. In actual fact, I work side by side with a shaman, because plants that produce chemicals are usually the most important medicinal plants; and they are also the plants that insects do not wish to eat!

One of my favorite discoveries was a new species of beetle that feeds only on one bromeliad living high in the Peruvian rain forest canopy. This beetle makes a characteristic racing-stripe damage along the leaf surfaces, so it is always obvious when it has been chewing. My two boys, Eddie and James, have been lifelong field assistants in my jungle explorations. They spent many long nights in the canopies of the Amazon with me, searching for this beetle. We finally found it in the act of consuming the bromeliad – such observations are necessary to confirm which herbivore is eating which plant. I studied this interaction during a global

distance learning programme called the Jason Project, working with Bob Ballard (the oceanographer who became obsessed with finding the wreck of the Titanic). Thousands of middle-school kids had a naming competition when we discovered this beetle on the show. The winning name was nutmeg beetle: for its color (nutmeg brown), for the nutmeg tree in which the bromeliad inhabited, and for the person who discovered it!

As a relatively new type of planetary exploration, canopy research has been ninety five per cent sweat equity and five per cent intellect, or at least sometimes it feels that way. Having solved the rudiments of access, scientists now focus on teasing apart the ecology of these forests, in order to understand their complex interactions. Like a doctor diagnoses human health, an ecologist measures and diagnoses change in ecosystems. Ecologists consider it critical to collect baseline ecological data to understand the health of our planet and predict change. Similarly, doctors keep records of our temperature, blood pressure, and other baseline data in order to best diagnose and treat human illness. Throughout years of canopy research, I have been assisted by hundreds, if not thousands, of explorers-in-training. Earthwatch volunteers, college

Sampling the canopy from a blimp.

students, high school students and their teachers, elementary and middle school students, fellow scientists and citizen scientists have donned harnesses, lassoed a branch with my slingshot, and measured thousands of leaves and insects as part of the process to learn about life above the forest floor.

Specifically, my long-term research involves plant-insect interactions. It is a beetle-eat-leaf world up there, oftentimes noisy at night with millions of foliage-feeding insects (termed herbivores) chomping on millions of leaves of trees, vines and air plants. This process of herbivory can lead to pest outbreaks, an important applied outcome of this research. Since plants cannot run away from enemies, leaves have evolved different strategies to defend themselves: thorns, hairs, poisonous chemicals, and toughness. The interaction of insects eating plants actually stimulates the production of chemicals in leaves and serves as a plant's major defence tactic. This response creates a veritable apothecary in the sky.

The living conditions of tropical expeditions are usually worthy of tall tales upon return. My favorite rainforest on the planet is the Amazon basin. Despite the lack of electricity or hot water showers, biologists enjoy the luxury of surround-sound biodiversity noises, thatch-roof huts, and local fresh fish every day. Often the only female present during some expedition, I hope that more young women will consider careers in field biology.

During almost 30 years of treetop exploration, I have whittled away at relatively small goals – one tree at a time. I can only hope that my scientific research will strengthen conservation and education about our planet's last remaining wild places for the next generation. The Amazon rainforests remain our last, best hope for conservation of both biodiversity and also the ecosystem services that keep our planet healthy. As a scientist and explorer, I have managed to discover a few new species; pioneered some new

methods of canopy access that opened some new frontiers in forest ecology; left a modest legacy of treetop walks encircling the globe to encourage ecotourism instead of chainsaws; and shared my exploration with kids through the wonders of distance learning. In my other role as a parent and explorer, I use my canopy exploration as an opportunity to connect my children to nature, and to remind them that human health links directly to the environment, not to computer screens or cellphones. Children need to get muddy, explore outdoors, and to understand that we are all part of our ecosystem, not outside of it. By advocating this ethic, both parents and scientists alike can impart environmental ethics to the next generation.

The greatest exploration remaining in the tropical treetops is perhaps not to map the last remaining remote jungles or climb the tallest trees. The most urgent exploration, with rewards far exceeding the discovery of a new beetle or a lost city, is to discover the secrets of how these complex ecological machines called rainforests function. It is a race against time. Our children and grandchildren depend upon the success of our exploration to unravel the ecological mysteries in our home, planet Earth. Many challenges remain in our exploration of the world's tropical jungles. We do not yet know the commonest tree in the Amazon, nor do we have any idea how many creatures live in a cubic meter of foliage. Yet we know the chemicals that compose Mars, the structure of an electron, and the genetic make-up of a mosquito. Science has advanced in many arenas, but the ability to understand the machinery of our "home" is still lacking. The exploration and scientific advances in canopy biology over the next twenty years are critical to understanding the health of forests that regulate the quality of life on our planet. For my children's sake, I hope we can expand planetary explorations out on a limb, and use our scientific results to generate sound conservation policies.

Pachira Aquatica

The plumage of the scarlet macaw

At first I thought I was fighting to save rubber trees, then I thought I was fighting to save the Amazon rainforest. Now I realise I am fighting for humanity.

- Chico Mendes (1944-88)

Brazilian rubber-tapper and environmental activist

Factfile

Some of the notable rivers and their lengths in the Amazon basin

Amazon, South America	6,762 km
Purus, Peru/Bolivia	3,379 km
Madeira, Bolivia/Brazil	3,239 km
Yapura, Colombia/Brazil	2,820 km
Tocantins, Brazil	2,750 km
Araguia, Brazil	2,575 km
Jurua, Peru/Brazil	2,410 km
Negro, South America	2,250 km
Xingu, Brazil	2,100 km
Tapajos, Brazil	1,900 km
Guapore, Brazil	1,749 km
Ka (Putumayo), Brazil	1,575 km
Maranon, Peru	1,415 km
Iriri, Brazil	1,300 km
Juruena, Brazil	1,240 km
Tapajos, Brazil	1,200 km
Madre de Dios, Peru/Bolivia	1,130 km
Huallaga, Peru	1,100 km

A Satellite map of the mouth of the Amazon river.

AMAZON RAINFOREST FACTS

○ The Amazon rainforest, the largest rainforest in the world, spans more than 2,375,000 sq km across nine Latin American countries.

○ The produce of at least 1,650 rainforest plants can be utilized as alternatives to our present fruit and vegetable staples

○ Starting its journey from the Andes mountains in Peru, the Amazon flows west to east across South America, roughly parallel to the Equator. It covers a distance of 6450 km before reaching the Atlantic Ocean in north-eastern Brazil.

○ A hectare (2.471 acres) of rainforest absorbs one ton of carbon dioxide (CO_2) per year. Clearing and burning of the rainforest accounts for 20-25% of the CO_2 emitted into the atmosphere by man, significantly contributing to the 'greenhouse effect'.

○ The Amazon rainforest receives an average of 203.2cm of annual rainfall. Comparatively, Cherrapunji in north-eastern India, considered the wettest place on earth, receives 279.4cm of annual rainfall.

○ It is estimated that 18,000 sq km of rainforest is lost annually – or approximately 137 species of diversity per day

Although vast expanse of Amazonia has escaped major industrial pollution, the greed for oil and minerals is affecting the biodiversity and ecological balance.

AMAZONIAN DIVERSITY

○ The Andean mountain range and the Amazon jungle are home to more than half the world's species of flora and fauna

○ Biodiversity in a typical 3 sq km area of the Amazon rainforest roughly includes 1,500 species of flowering plants, 750 species of trees, 125 species of mammals, 400 species of birds, 100 species of reptiles, 60 species of amphibians, and 150 species of butterflies.

○ There are more fish species in the Amazon river system than in the entire Atlantic Ocean

○ A single rainforest reserve in Peru is home to more species of birds than the entire United States. At least a third of the planet's bird species lives in the Amazon rainforest

○ 37% of all medicines prescribed in the Unites States have active ingredients derived from rainforest plants (45% of the world's prescription medicines are derived from rainforest plants)

○ 70% of the plant species identified by the US National Cancer Institute as having anti-cancer properties comes from rainforests. 90% of the rainforest plants used by Amazonian Indians as medicines have not been examined by modern science.

○ Of the few rainforest plant species that have been studied by modern medicine, treatments have been found for juvenile leukemia, breast cancer, high blood pressure, asthma and scores of other illnesses.

○ 6-9 million indigenous people inhabited the Brazilian rainforest in 1500. In 1992, less than 200,000 remained.

○ In the Amazon basin, nearly 1.5 million people constitute 400 different tribes/ethnicity groups.

A decomposer in the Rainforest is a fungus type organism, such as mushrooms.

○ Some of the kinds of employment people are involved in the Amazon basin are farming and ranching, gold mining, rubber tapping, fishing, hunting/gathering, oil industry, lumber industry, tourism and service industries.

Amazonia: A treasure trove of medicinal plants

The Amazonia can be considered the richest natural bio-fermentor on the planet, a virtual library of biochemical invention. In these archives are present drugs like quinine, muscle relaxants, steroids and cancer drugs. More importantly, new drugs could be awaiting discovery – drugs for AIDS, cancer, diabetes, arthritis and Alzheimer's. The wealth of medicinal knowledge possessed by the indigenous people of the rainforest is now thought to be the Amazon's new gold. Indians and indigenous people have used these herbal concoctions for their survival, health and well-being from time immemorial.

Some Plants and their Medicinal Values

ABUTA (Cissampelos pareira)	Antispasmodic, antihemorrhagic (reduces bleeding), muscle relaxant, uterine relaxant, hypotensive (lowers blood pressure)
ANDIROBA (Carapa guianensis)	Analgesic (plain reliever), anti-inflammatory, insect repellent, anti-tumorous, wound-healer
ARTICHOKE (Cynara scolymus)	Liver and gallbladder bile stimulant, hepatoprotective (liver protector), antithepatoxic (liver detoxifier), hypocholesterolemic (lowers cholestrol)
BITTER MELON leaf / stem (Momordica charantia)	Anticancerous, antiviral, antibacterial, digestive stimulant, hypoglycemic
BRAZIL NUT (Bertholletia excelsa)	Nutritive, antioxidant, emollient
CATUABA (Erythroxylum catuaba)	Aphrodisiac, nervine (balances/calms nerves)anti-anxiety, central nervous system tonic (tones, balances, strengthens the nervous system), anti viral
FEDEGOSO (Cassia occidentalis)	Antimicrobial, antithepatotoxic (liver detoxifier), hepatotonic (tones, balances, strengthens the liver), antiparasitic, immune stimulant
MACA (Lepidum meyenii)	Tonic (tones, balances, strengthens overall body functions), nutritive, fertility enhancer, endocrine function support, anti-fatigue
PASSIONFLOWER (Passiflora incarnata)	Antidepresent, analgesic (pain-reliever), antispasmodic, sedative, central nervous system depressant
PEDRA HUME CAA (Myrcia salicifolia)	Antidiabetic, hypolglycemic, aldose reductase inhabitor (prevents diabetic complications), astringent, hypotensive (lowers blood pressure)
QUININE (Cinchona sp.)	Anti malarial, bitter digestive aid, antiparasitic, antispasmodic, febrifuge (reduces fever)
VELVET BEAN (Mucuna pruriens)	Anti-Parkinson's, androgenic, aphrodisiac, hypoglycemic, anabolic
YERBA MATE (Ilex paraguariensis)	Stimulant, tonic (tones, balances, strengthens over all body functions), thermogenic (increase fat burning), nervine (balances/calm nerves), anti-allergy

First used by local tribes, the açai berry is rich in carbohydrates, vitamins, minerals, proteins and fat, and is used to fight ageing, boost energy, improve vision, strengthen the heart and stimulate the brain.

River dolphins are found in large numbers in both the Amazon and the Orinoco river systems.

The famed pink dolphins of the Amazon owe their colour to the waters: The darker the water, the pinker the dolphin.

The black caiman is the largest predator in the Amazon river. Also called jacaré, it averages 10-13ft in length, and is found east of the Andes to the Atlantic, and north of the Brazilian Pantanal to southern Venezuela. Apart from aquatic species, they ambush terrestrial animals, particularly capybara, but also vulnerable peccaries and tapirs.

Travel & Photography

"We shall not ccase from exploration
And the end of all our exploring
Will be to arrive where we started
And know the place for the first time."

- T.S. Eliot

Sometimes the river is just too tempting for local travelers, who have been known to jump off the boats for a swim.

Transportation in Amazonia:

*T*ravel in the great Amazon basin is an incredible experience by itself. However, there are only two modes of transportation here: Either you journey down the river in a boat or you fly above the canopy of the rainforest. Both the boat and the helicopter offer enough excitement to keep you mesmerized.

Another thing to keep in mind while preparing to travel in the Amazonia is that there are only two seasons in the rainforest: It's either raining or 'dry'. The months from December to July receive the most rainfall, while the remaining months see occasional spells of rain – thereby qualifying them to be 'dry' in local parlance! It's never completely dry in the Amazonia. So whatever you do, don't forget to pack your umbrella and raincoat.

Negotiating the waterways:

The Amazon ticks to its own time. No matter what the pace of life may be in Brazil's big cities, on the Amazon a stretch of 400 km can take around 27 hours to travel. Rivers are the superhighways of this country, providing an experience similar to sailing in the backwaters of Kerala in India. No buses ply through the jungles of the Amazon basin – which is also one reason why no bridge crosses the river.

Like long train trips, boat journeys can sometimes turn out to be leisure excursions. The mood on board is usually easy and friendly, and time flies with beer and conversation. There's almost always Brazilian music and dance on the deck and, if that's too demanding for you, join in one of the innumerable card games that seem to be played all across the boat.

Else, there's always much to feast your eyes on: The simple lives of the river people can make for unforgettable images, both for the memory and for the camera. And if you are an artist, there's inspiration around every corner on this journey through the Amazonian landscape: It has no parallels anywhere in the world.

But it's not all about going with the flow. Every traveller has to be perpetually on the lookout for thieves, an unfortunate fallout of the high levels of unemployment in the country. Be especially careful of your luggage and gear near ports, where scores of boats may be anchored.

Also, keep in mind that the facilities on board boats that ply the Amazon are usually extremely basic. Individual private cabins with air-conditioning are occasionally available on regular boats, and will guarantee both clean toilets and safety for your gear. A few luxury boats also do the

A boat can be used for work - or play.

Amazon trip, but one could easily fly between the main cities – and lose out on the beautiful riverbank vistas – for the rates they charge.

Boats usually have three decks. The top deck is meant for hanging out with pals and has a dance floor blasting music round-the-trip. The other two decks are meant for hammocks, the commonest way of marking space and ensuring a night's rest. If you can, use a mosquito net, in the boat and later, while camping.

Brazil is a liberal society when it comes to relationships between the sexes, and it's a definite advantage if you speak the national language, Portuguese. However, bear in mind that the Portuguese spoken in Europe and the one spoken in Brazil are very diffcrent.

One of the fun elements of my travel down the Amazon was the rediscovery of hammocks. It's customary for everyone to rig up their hammock and curl up for the night. I still have mine as a souvenir.

Whatever the setting, there's always scope for some music and dance.

Living on the Amazon

The Amazonian jungles are very humid, with an equatorial climate and very heavy rainfall. As anywhere else, dress for the weather in the Amazonia – and also be alive to pests such as mosquitoes and other biting insects, snakes and leeches. Carry long trousers, long-sleeved shirts, shady hats and tough shoes. Don't forget mosquito-repellent creams and basic medicines for fever, allergy or bad tummies. Medical facilities are expensive and not easily available. A yellow fever shot is a must before you hit the region.

No meal is complete in Brazil without meat: Locals eat rice, beans and meat three times a day. This might pose a big problem for vegetarianos! There is, usually, however, a good supply of fruits and potatoes. In the boats, water is a major constraint. Hygienic drinking water is rare to find unless the boats are carrying bottled water. Always carry iodine capsules to add to the water before drinking.

If you're fond of swimming, go right ahead, without worrying about your attire! It is common to see locals take a dip in the river in whatever they are wearing. Go along and follow suit: It makes for a

Anytime is a good time for a dip in the Amazon.

thrilling experience – and the wet clothes dry in no time. One should, however, be on the lookout for piranhas and alligators. Also, the mercury levels in the river are a cause for concern.

In the forests

A word of advice for amateur wildlife enthusiasts: The Amazon rainforest is serious jungle, not a set for a reality show. Never take things for granted. An innocent scratch mark or two from an animal could have dangerous repercussions. Carry a first-aid kit and move only in groups.

Most species of flora and fauna in the Amazon basin are listed as endangered and endemic. So don't even think of hunting them or taking a specimen back home as a souvenir.

Brazilian cuisine is meat heavy.

Photographing the Amazonia

The Amazon basin is a photographer's delight. Although there is no single correct method or perfect way to take pictures, the Amazon opens up a world of opportunities for taking photos of extraordinary diversity and dimensions. A great picture that captures the enduring beauty of the land is usually the combination of perfect lighting, an artistic mind and creative composition. Above all, rainforest photography needs large quantities of dedication, patience, creativity and a love of fieldwork.

Even with the rest in place, one can never be certain of perfect lighting conditions in the Amazonia. And that is the greatest challenge for any photographer.

The flooded forest poses enormous challenges for maneuvering but offers great opportunities for the observant traveller. Only unreasonable expectations can disappoint a visitor.

Guarana is an Amazonian native shrub, found in Brazil and Venezuela. Its fruit contains a substance similar to caffeine, because of which it finds use in the manufacture of syrups and soft drinks.

The Pequi is a fruit used in many different ways: It is eaten with rice and pasta, cooked with chicken and fish. When bottled, its syrup forms a crystal, which some regard as an aphrodisiac.

*The Negro is well-known for its unique physio-chemical characteristics,
created by a very high content of dissolved organic matter.*

Camouflaged Green Iguana

The white caiman lives in lowland and riverine habitats, helped by its tolerance to salt water. It is often called the 'spectacled' caiman, because of the high bony ridge between the eyes and the eyebrow ridges can look vaguely like a pair of glasses.

River: The river itself is so majestic that one can record it endlessly. Its characteristic colours, which change over the course of its journey from the Andes to the Atlantic, are a mute challenge to the photographic eye to capture it in its original state and spirit.

People: The riverine people are a joyous lot and throw up many chances for creative photography. By isolating a subject, one can define very strong characters in the photographs. Composing pictures in this delightful odyssey has more to do with presence of mind than merely clicking the shutter on what one sees through the eyepiece of the camera.

Rainforest: In the forest and the surroundings, use ISO 200 and above, flash cards or transparencies. Inside the forests, light is never uniform and never hits the forest floor. One has to make the most of the rare occasions when light penetrates through the canopy. While in the forest, always be ready to act. Be warned that there will be few opportunities that you can anticipate in these jungles. Wildlife sightings, rare in themselves, are very, very difficult to record, but the least you can do is be ready. Although no two pairs of eyes will see the Amazonia the same way, a perceptive mind can open hidden gateways to bring out the astounding beauty of this land.

Light: While appropriate lighting is an important component of any good picture, one needs to keep a few factors in mind in view of the scanty light that filters through the forest canopy. Lighting conditions tend to be uniform along the riverbank, and plenty of macro work can be undertaken in these areas. At the same time, one has to keep an eye out for reptiles lurking beneath the leaf litter or animal species camouflaged in the foliage. On the riverside, keep an eye out for changing light patterns and dramatic landscapes. Storm clouds and the river make for great photos. In a matter of minutes, colours can change dramatically, lending whole new looks to the landscape.

The Amazon allows for every kind of photography: Nature, landscape, aerial, or people. Presence of mind, the right decisions on the equipment and the composition will turn out to make the difference between a great photo and a

The sun sets on the Pará river across from Belém

mediocre one. Attune your eyes to both a binocular and a macroscopic vision to make most of the excellent opportunities that present themselves.

Protecting your camera: Always guard your equipment from water and thieves. Carry good protective covers for your gear. Humidity is an important factor to always keep in mind. While travelling by boat, carry an extra plastic cover or suitable covering material to protect your equipment from splashes of water.

While walking in the forest, do not carry much gear. It not only restricts your movement but it also doesn't make much sense, as forest conditions will not allow you to use many different kinds of lenses or accessories.

It's advisable to carry a spare set of equipment: Remember, the longer you expose one piece of camera equipment to the humidity, the more the chances of fungal growth (and there are no repair shops anywhere near the rainforests).

Always be careful about photographing in isolation. In the Amazon basin, always be on guard, especially in the port cities. Do not leave any equipment unattended anywhere. Always carry a bag that will allow you to organize your equipment for easy accessibility. Do not forget to charge your batteries before you start for the day. Carry back the exposed film to a trusted place after the shoot. If you are travelling for a prolonged stretch, be careful about the innumerable X-rays that the films go through at the airports.

The Brazilian Amazonia is home to more than 4,000 species of butterflies. This Butterfly belongs to the Pieridade family, part of the native fauna of the Sierra Capivara.

Equipment used to photograph the pictures in this book:

Nikon F5 camera body with NiMH Battery unit

Nikon D100 camera body with MB-D100 Vertical Grip/ Battery Holder

Nikon D300 camera body with MB-D300 Vertical Grip/ Battery Holder

Nikkor 300mm f/4 IF-ED AF-S

Nikkor 80-200 mm f/2.8 IF-ED AF

Nikkor 24-85 mm f/3.5-4.5 G ED-IF AF-S

Nikkor SB-28 DX compact flash

Nikkor 70-180 mm f/4.5-5.6 AF

Nikon SB-29S Macro speed light

Nikon SU-4 Wireless remote TTL Flash controller

Nikon TC-20E II (2x) AF-S, AF-I teleconverter

Nikon TC-14E II (1.4x) AF-S, AF-I teleconverter

Camera cleaning accessories (cleaning fluids, Nikon lens cleaning cloth, blower brush)

Jewelers screw driver set & needle nose pliers

Gitzo Mountaineer carbon fibre tripod G1348

Gitzo centre ball heads with quick release plate

Lowepro Photo trekker AW II

Lowepro Orion trekker

Fujifilm RDP-III 135-36 Provia 100 F Professional Color slide

Kodak GB 135-36 Gold 200 color print film

Lexar 1GB / 2 GB / 4 GB compact flash card

Please don't think you need all the listed equipment to photograph in the Amazon wilderness. All you need would be one good camera, lens and a photographic eye!

Epilogue

When I set out to explore the wilderness of the Amazonia, my heart was filled with a multitude of emotions. I was excited, nervous and expectant, all at the same time. When I landed in Brazil, I felt very much at home in my surroundings. I could not wait to step into the rainforests, something that I looked forward to every minute ever since my Brazil plans were initiated. And on first encounter, the rainforests and the mighty Amazon simply overwhelmed me with their magnificence. Slowly, my eyes became accustomed to the vast stretches of greenery and I began to feel comfortable on the mighty river as well. After my initial excitement died down, I got down to capturing the beauty and mystery of the Amazonia on film.

As a natural history photographer, my goal has always been to capture images of nature that evoke emotion and inspire my audience. I went around the jungles of the Amazonia documenting the not-so-obvious wildlife and vibrant greenery. Even then, I planned to present them to my audience in a form that enthused them to learn more about these threatened landscapes, the equally threatened wildlife, the indigenous people of the land and their cultures. I sincerely hope that my photographs and the accompanying narrative will help in both understanding and appreciating nature's gifts to humanity and driving home the urgency of protecting the threatened landscapes of our planet.

Time Line: Brazil

90Mil BC	The *Baurusuchus salgadoensis* lived in an area of south-eastern Brazil known as the Bauru Basin, some 700 km (450 miles) west of modern-day Rio de Janeiro. The fossilized skeletons appear to be closely related to another ancient crocodile species, the *Pabwehshi pakistanesis*, discovered in Pakistan.
48000 BC	Charcoal from camp fires in the Pedra Furada site of Piaui state were carbondated to about this time in 1987.
9500 BC	A skull of a female, aged 20-25, from about this time was found near Belo Horizonte around 1995. Named Luzia, it had characteristics similar to those of people from the South Pacific
1500	Jan 26. Spanish explorer Vicente Yáñez Pinzón reached the northeastern coast of Brazil during a voyage under his command. Pinzón had commanded the ship Niña during Christopher Columbus's first expedition to the New World
1500	April 22. Pedro Álvares Cabral (c1460-c1526), Portuguese explorer, discovered Brazil and claimed it for Portugal. He anchored for 10 days in a bay he called Porto Seguro before continuing on to India
1501	Jan 1. Cabral returned with Italian explorer Amerigo Vespucci and sailed into Guanabara Bay and, mistaking it for the mouth of a river, named it Rio de Janeiro.
1502	Portuguese traders took peanuts from Brazil and Peru to Africa
1542	Aug 24. Spanish conquistador Gonzalo Pizarro returned to the mouth of the Amazon after sailing up the length of the great river as far as the Andes mountains
1543	Sugar cane was introduced to Brazil around this time. Fermented sugar cane later became the base for Cachaça, a light rum, which later became the base for the national drink, the Caipirinha.
1550	African slaves were shipped to Brazil to work in the sugar plantations
1600-1700	Brazil's Ouro Preto (Black Gold in Portuguese) was founded in the 17th century after huge gold deposits were discovered under its steep hills
1624	The Dutch conquered Salvador
1641	Cristóbal de Acuna, a Jesuit missionary from Spain, wrote about the Amazon river to the king of Spain. This is the first time the outside world learnt about the river.
1661	Aug 6. Holland sold Brazil to Portugal for 8 million guilders
1727	Brazil planted its first coffee
1730	Diamonds were discovered in Brazil. It was the world's leading supplier of the gemstone till the 1866 discovery in South Africa
1763	The capital of Brazil moved from Salvador to Rio de Janeiro
1819	Johann Baptist von Spix discovered the Spix Macaw of Brazil (*Cyanopsitta spixii*), one of the four species of blue macaws ever known
1822	Sept 7. Brazil declared its independence from Portugal
1873	Britain sent an agent, Henry Wickham, to Brazil to get rubber seeds. The seedlings were cultivated in Kew Gardens and transported to Malaysia
1888	Slavery was abolished. Large influx of European immigrants over the next decade
1912	Explorer Algot Lange authored *In the Amazon Jungle* after a 1910 expedition in the upper Amazon, which he survived only with the aid of Mangeroma cannibals

1931	Oct 12. The 28.9m statue of Christ the Redeemer was unveiled atop the Corcovado Mountain. Today it is one of the major icons of Brazil.
1960	April 21. Brasilia was declared the new capital of Brazil, as national government moved away from Rio de Janeiro
1965	Peru cut a trail through the Amazonian jungle to Iñapari, its border town across from Assis, Brazil
1978	July 3. Brazil initiated the Amazon Pact to coordinate the development of the Amazon basin. It was signed by Bolivia, Brazil, Colombia, Ecuador, Guyana, Peru, Suriname and Venezuela.
1978-1996	Over 200,000 sq. miles, 12.5% of the rainforest, was destroyed.
1991	The Amazon forest lost 3 million acres this year. Four years later, another 7 million acres had disappeared.
1996-2000	Deforestation of the Amazon region reached 5 million acres per year
1997	Oct 29. It was reported that at least 10% of the 2 million square-mile Amazon basin was destroyed by fire
1998	Worst drought since 1983 in Northeastern Brazil, one of the prime regions of the Amazonia.
1998	Oct 7. The Spix Macaw, now identified as the world's largest wild bird, was valued at $60,000 in the animal trafficking market; in another couple of years, it would be extinct. 218 species in Brazil were declared endangered, including 109 birds, 68 mammals, 31 invertebrates, 9 reptiles and 1 amphibian.
2002	June 30. Brazil defeated Germany in the football world cup final to win the title for an unprecedented fifth time
2005	Parts of the Amazon river in Brazil was declared disaster zone as the water level dropped too low to allow navigation
2020	Deforestation of the Amazon region is expected to reach 28-42%

Source: timeline.ws

A quiet boat journey along the backwaters of the Amazon River in the late evening is one of the best times to be surprised by the amazing wildlife.

Bibliography

1. Agassiz, Louis; Agassiz, Elizabeth Cabot Cary. *A Journey in Brazil*. Boston: Tucknor and Fields. Out of copyright.

2. Smith, Nigel; Vasquez, Rodolfo; Wust, Walter H. *Amazon River Fruits: Flavors for Conservation*. St Louis, MO: Amazon Conservation Association; Missouri Botanical Garden Press. 2007.

3. Castner, J. L.; Timme, S. L.; Duke, J.A. *A Field Guide to Medicinal and Useful Plants of the Upper Amazon*. Gainesville, FL: Feline Press, 1988.

4. Duke, J.A.; Vasquez, R. *Amazonian Ethnobotanical Dictionary*. Boca Raton, FL: CRC Press, 1994.

5. Castner, James L.; Timme, Stephen L.; Duke, James A. *A Field Guide to Medicinal and Useful Plants of the Upper Amazon*. Gainesville, FL: Feline Press, 1988.

6. Gentry, A.H.A. *A Field Guide to the Families and Genera of Woody Plants of Northwest South America*. Washington, DC: Conservation International, 1993.

7. Henderson, A. *The Palms of the Amazon*. Oxford: Oxford University Press, 1995.

8. Henderson, A.; Galeano, G; Bernal, R. *A Field Guide to the Palms of the Americas*. Princeton, NJ: Princeton University Press, 1995.

9. Kricher, J.C. *A Neotropical Companion*. Princeton, NJ: Princeton University Press, 1997.

10. Mejia, K.; Rengifo, E. *Plantas Medicinales de Uso Popular en la Amazonia Peruana*. Lima, Peru: Agencia Espanola de Cooperacion Internacional and Instituto de Investigaciones de la Amazonia Peruana, 1995.

11. Padoch, C.; Ayres, J.M; Pinedo-Vasquez, M; Henderson, A. *Varzea: Diversity, Development, and Conservation of Amazonia's Whitewater Floodplain*. New York, NY: New York Botanical Garden Press, 1988.

12. Colinvaux, Paul. *Amazon Expeditions: My Quest for the Ice-Age Equator*. London: Yale University Press, 2008.

13. Roosevelt, T. *Through the Brazilian Wilderness*. New York, NY: Cooper Square Press, 1914.

14. Schleser, D.M. *Piranhas*. Hauppauge, NY: Barron's Educational Series, Inc., 1997.

15. Sioli, H. *The Amazon. Limnology and Landscape Ecology of a Mighty Tropical River and its Basin*. Dordrecht, The Netherlands: Dr W. Junk Publishers, 1984.

16. Smith, A. *Explorers of the Amazon*. Chicago, IL: The University of Chicago Press, 1990.

17. Smith, N.J.H. *The Amazon River Forest: A Natural History of Plants, Animals, and People*. Oxford: Oxford University Press, 1999.

18. Smith, N.J.H. *The Enchanted Amazon Rainforest*. Gainesville, FL: University Press of Florida, 1996.

19. Schultes, Richard Evans; Raffauf, Robert F. *The Healing Forest: Medicinal and Toxic Plants of the Northwest Amazonia*. Portland, OR: Dioscorides Press, 1990.

20. Davis, Wade. *One River: Explorations and Discoveries in the Amazon Rain Forest.* New York, NY: Simon and Schuster, 1996.

21. Anderson, A.B. *Alternatives to Deforestation: Steps toward Sustainable Use of the Amazon Rainforest.* New York, NY: Columbia University Press, 1990

22. Bates, H.W. *The Naturalist on the River Amazon; A Record of Adventures, Habitat of Animals, Sketches of Brazilian and Indian Life, and Aspects of Nature Under the Equator, During the Eleven Years of Travel.* London: J. Murray, 1863.

23. Charnela, J.M. *The Wanano Indians of the Brazilian Amazon.* Austin, TX: University of Texas Press, 1993.

24. Daly, D.C., and Prance, G.T. Prance. *Brazilian Amazon.* New York: New York Botanical Garden Press, 1989.

25. Lisoba, P.L.B. *Caxiuanã.* Belém, Brazil: Museu Paranese Emílio Goeldi, 1997

26. Malhi, Yadvinder; Phillips, Oliver. *Tropical Forests and Global Atmospheric Change.* Oxford: Oxford University Press, 2005.

27. Smith, N.J.H. *The Amazon River Forest: A Natural History of Plants, Animals, and People.* Oxford: Oxford University Press, 1999.

28. Smith, N.J.H. *Amazon Sweet Sea: Land, Life, and Water at the River's Mouth.* Austin, TX: University of Texas Press, 2002.

29. Thurm, Everard im; Cairn Hodge, A.; Walkey, O.R.; Williams, James; Rice, Hamilton. "Further Explorations in the North-West Amazon Basin." *The Geographical Journal,* Vol. 44, No. 2, 1914. 164-168.

30. Goulding, Michael; Ferreira, E.J.G. *"Shrimp-eating fishes and a case of prey-switching in Amazon Rivers."* Revista Brasileira de Zoologia, Vol. 2, No. 3, 1983. 85-97

31. Junk, W.J; Ohly, J.J.; Piedade, M.T.F.; Soares, M.G.M. (eds). *The Central Amazon Floodplain: Actual Use and Options for a Sustainable Management.* Leiden, The Netherlands: Backhuys. 2000.

32. Reynolds, Jay. *The Amazon basin: Vanishing Cultures.* Mooloolaba, Australia. Sandpiper publications, 1993

33. Lowman, Margaret D. *Life in the Treetops: Adventures of a Woman in Field Biology.* New Haven, CT: Yale University Press, 1999.

34. Webb, Alex. *Amazon: From the Floodplains to the Clouds.* New York, NY: Monacelli, 1998.

35. Pearson, L. David; Beletsky, Les. "Brazil: Amazon And Pantanal." *Travellers' Wildlife Guides,* Northampton, MA: Interlink books, 2005.

36. Wilson, David J. *Indigenous South Americans of the Past and Present: An Ecological Perspective.* Boulder, CO: Westview Press, 1999.

37. Steward, Julian H; Faron, Louis C. *Native Peoples of South America.* New York, NY: McGraw-Hill Press, 1959.

Acknowledgements

I do not work alone. A number of scholars, professionals and friends have helped me in my quest to acquire knowledge and capture compelling images of the diversity of our home planet. This is my effort to humbly acknowledge each one of them for their unstinting support.

My first respects must go to Dr Yadvinder Malhi, Professor of Ecosystem Science at the University of Oxford. This book is the outcome of the opportunity Dr Malhi offered me to work with him in the Brazilian Amazonia. His constant support and confidence in my capabilities made this endeavor possible. I am indebted to him for making my dream a reality.

Dr Oliver Phillips was a source of great encouragement and enthusiasm, constantly providing me information about plant species, native Amazonian culture and the Amazonian environment. His company was a boon on my visits to Caxiuanã.

In Brazil, over a period of time I have enjoyed the hospitality and support of many people, each of whom contributed in making impossible situations easier. I am deeply grateful to them all, especially Samuel Almeida and his family, whose efforts to feed "the vegetariano" is something I will never forget. I also thank Jorge, Flavia, Debora, Pedro, Elen and Dinai for their extraordinary hospitality and warmth.

Dr Ima Viera, former director of Meseu Goeldi, took a personal interest in my work and shared information and resources to facilitate my visit to the Marajó islands. I thank her for all her help. I made several visits to the deep Amazonia with Luiz Aragáo, my favorite Brazilian in spirit and action. He not only showed me how to survive the rainforest, but was a great companion in the deep heart of the Amazonia. I wish to thank Lianna Anderson and Rosa Mary for helping me bridge the Portuguese language barrier and identify species and for waiting for hours with me over the canopies at sunrise and sunset around Caxiuanã. Their enthusiasm pepped me up even as I wilted under my heavy equipment bag. Ana Claudia's child-like interest in the Amazonian way of life was like a tonic of great motivation. Besides her help in the field, she willingly contributed a chapter on sustainability in the Amazonia. I thank her for all the help. Thanks also go out to Antonio Sergio, Carlos Rosario and Dario Danhas for their good company, cachaça on the river and great cheer.

When I wanted a chapter on the Amazonian canopy, I couldn't think of anyone other than the canopy lady, Dr Meg Lowan. She accepted my request in two minutes flat. Her chapter is invaluable for a better understanding of the green ocean, the Amazonia. Thank you Meg for the special inputs you gave this book.

The Embassy of Brazil in India has been very appreciative of my work in the Amazon. Their invitation to exhibit my photographs further motivated me to complete this book. I thank his Excellency, former Ambassador of Brazil in India Jose Vicente Pimentel for his encouragement and support. I also thank Blanche Gomes and Ritu Bhaktiani at the embassy for their extended help.

I owe a large dept of gratitude to Dr Jasbir and Lori Sra of Wisconsin for their invaluable support through my journey. I remember Dr Kapil Bhalla and Kathy Bhalla for their continued indulgence of my obsession with natural history photography.

There are many friends without whom this book would never have materialized. My special thanks to every one of them: Rudresh Babu, the man for all seasons, who never says no whatever I may call him for; Praveen Siddarth, my best buddy, my biggest fan and a great source of encouragement always; Raman Babu, who not only engaged in environmental discussions but helped with resources on request. I wholeheartedly thank Dr Madhav Badanhatti and Dr Ravi Prakash and their families in the UK for their technical inputs, engaging photographic conversations, constant encouragement, help and support.

Nature photography might be a challenging occupation, but it makes for challenges in one's personal life as well, necessitating constrained circumstances by way of money and time for family. My parents have always been one of my greatest sources of

support and inspiration. Their never-say-die spirit makes me stride forward with optimism and positivity. I thank them for instilling in me the confidence and the spirit of adventure. One person who has to bear first-hand my obsession with photography and my constant travels is my dear wife, Rekha. Her unfailing good cheer brings out the best in me in all situations. I thank her for making my homecoming so special, every single time. I sincerely thank Bhargav and Raghuveer Rao for taking pride in my work and for their timely help with resources.

This book took a decisive shape because of the efforts of my editor and dear friend Sumana Mukherjee. Her inputs in giving form to my random thoughts were invaluable. My special thanks to her.

Talented designer R Srinath converted my manuscript into a beautiful illustrated book with his creative inputs. I thank him for his insightful help.

It is with deep gratitude that I thank Frank and Jackie Christian. Their patience, enthusiasm and "come what may, make it happen" spirit has been one of the greatest inspirations.I wish to thank Dr. Pai and his family as well as my friends at Augusta for their rock solid support in my endeavors and passion. I thank my friends Tom and Mary Ann Grant, whose appreciation of my art has been one of the pillars of support in my quest for excellence. John Clouse at Nikon believed in my abilities and has been extremely supportive with resources and constant support for my passion. I sincerely thank him for all his help. My thanks to John H. K. Riley at Lowepro for his continued interest and support in my work.

On the river, boats and canoes of all sizes are a symbol of a lifestyle that has survived every kind of storm for centuries.

Index

Photo Credits

About the Authors

Harald Hansen

D.K. Bhaskar

With a serious interest in science and research, Bhaskar regularly collaborates with institutes in exploring the diversity of the natural world. A Fellow of The Explorers Club, in the course of his expeditions he has crisscrossed deserts, rainforests, mountain passes and the Arctic tundra.

He is the winner of several prestigious awards, including the Raleigh International Photographer of the Year (UK) and Gold Award in the Bill Muster Photo Showcase (USA). Additionally, he has been honored with the President's Scout Medal from His Excellency the President of India. He is also founder and vice-chairman of the Augusta Photo Festival, USA and president of International Photography Partnership.

In a career spanning a little over eight years, his photojournalistic features and stories have been published in leading magazines, books and journals, including *UNESCO Journal*, *BBC*, *Discovery*, *Insight Guides*, *Lonely Planet*, *Khabar*, *Podróze*, *Journal of Bio-geography*, *Mint*, *Popular Photography*, *Earthwatch*, *Wildlife Conservation Society*, *World Wildlife Fund* and *The Straits Times*. Seventeen books have used his work to illustrate monographs, stories and chapters. He is supported by Nikon, Lowepro and Datacolor. Website www.dewworks.com

Dr Yadvinder Malhi, Ph.D

Professor of Ecosystem Science at the School of Geography and the Environment and Programme Leader in Ecosystems at the Environmental Change Institute, his research interests centre around interactions between forest ecosystems and the global atmosphere, with a particular focus on their role in global carbon, energy and water cycles, and in understanding how the ecology of natural ecosystems may be shifting in response to global atmospheric change. More recently, his interests have expanded to include the impacts and limitation of tropical deforestation. He has been conducting field research in the forests of Amazonia for more than 15 years and has published over 75 scientific papers and 12 book chapters, and co-edited a book, *Tropical Forests and Global Atmospheric Change*.

He is a member of the Royal Society Advisory Committee on Climate Change and Ocean Acidification, the Royal Society Committee on Science in Society and the Scientific Steering Committee of the Large Scale Biosphere Atmosphere Experiment in Amazonia.

Dr Oliver Phillips, Ph.D

Professor of Tropical Ecology at the University of Leeds, his main research interests are in understanding the natural dynamics of tropical forests, especially the growth and death of forest trees, and how these natural processes are responding to our changing climate. He coordinates the 'RAINFOR' network of scientists from a dozen countries, who work together to record the behaviour of the Amazon rainforest. Through his 25 years of tropical research, Oliver has been fortunate to have worked alongside many extraordinary people who share his passion for the forest world.

Dr Meg Lowman, Ph.D

Director of Environmental Initiatives and Professor of Biology and Environmental Studies at the New College of Florida, she currently serves on the board of The Explorers Club. Her scientific text *Forest Canopies* was published in 2004 by Elsevier Publishers (ISBN 0-12-457553-6). Her next book, It's a *Jungle Out There – More Tales from the Treetops* (co-authored with her explorer-sons Edward and James Burgess, Yale University Press, 2006) chronicles their family exploration of forest canopies around the world, with case studies of combining exploration and research with conservation and education outreach.

Dr Ana Cláudia Mendes Malhado, Ph.D

An ecologist and science administrator, she is currently doing postdoctoral research on the ecology of forest ecosystems and their interaction with climate and hydrology at the Federal University of Viçosa, Brazil. She did her Ph.D from Oxford University in 2008. Her long term interest lies in contribution to the future economic, environmental, and social development of Brazil.

Resources

Amazon Conservation Association
1822 R St NW · Fourth Floor ·
Washington DC 20009 · USA
www.amazonconservation.org

Amazon Institute of People and the Environment (IMAZON)
Rua Domingos Marreiros, 2020
Fátima - Belém-Para -66060-160, Brazil
www.imazon.org.br

Conservation International
1919 M Street, NW Suite 600
Washington, DC 20036
www.conservation.org

CanopyMeg
Department of Environmental Studies
New College of Florida
5800 Bay Shore Road,
Sarasota, FL 34243
www.canopymeg.com

EMBRATUR - Instituto Brasileiro de Turismo
SCN Quadra 2 - Bloco G - 2º
andar - Brasília - DF
CEP: 70.712-907 - Brasil
www.braziltour.gov.br

Explorers Club
46 E. 70th Street ,
New York, NY 10021
www.explorers.org

Gitzo Tripods
www.gitzo.com

International Society for the Preservation of the Tropical Rainforest
3302 N Burton Avenue
Rosemead, California 91770 USA
www.istpr.org

International Union for Conservation of Nature (IUCN)
Rue Mauverney 28
Gland 1196
Switzerland
www.iucn.org

Large Scale Bioshpere-Atmosphere Experiment in Amazonia (LBA)
LBA-INPA
Av. Andŕe Araüjo, 2936
Alexio, Manaus, AM, CEP 69060-001
www.inpa.gov.br

Lowepro
1003 Gravenstein Highway North,
Suite 200, Sebastopol, CA 9547
www.lowepro.com

Museu Paraense Emilio Goeldi - MPEG
Av. Gov. Magalhaes Barata, 376
Belem-Para 66040-170, Brazil
http://www.museu-goeldi.br/

National Geographic Society
1145 17th Street, N.W.
Washington D.C. 20086 USA
www.nationalgeographic.com

Nikon Inc.
1300, Walt Whitman Road,
Melville, Ny-11747-3064 USA
www.nikon.com

Project for the Advancement of Networked Science in Amazonia (Pan-Amazonia)
School of Geography and the
Environment

University of Oxford
South Parks Road, Oxford,
OX1 3QY UK
www.pan-amazonia.org

Rainforest Foundation US
180 Varick Street, Suite 528
www.rainforestfoundation.org

RAINFOR
Amazon forest inventory Network
School of Geography,
University of Leeds,
Leeds, LS2 9JT, UK
www.rainfor.org

Smithsonian Institute
PO Box 37012
SI Building, Room 153, MRC 010
Washington, D.C. 20013
www.si.edu

World Wildlife Fund
1250 24th street, NW
Washington D.C. 20037 USA
www.wwf.org

and the eternal journey in Amazon continues to baffle explorers....